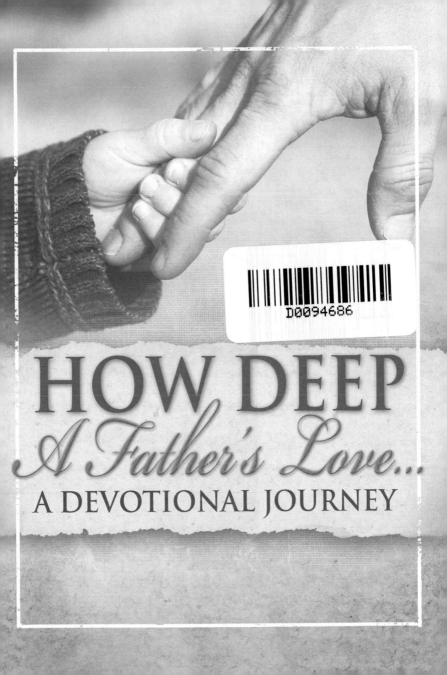

HOW DEEP
A Father's Love...
A DEVOTIONAL JOURNEY

Freeman-Smith, a division of Worthy Media, Inc.

134 Franklin Road, Suite 200, Brentwood, Tennessee 37027

The quoted ideas expressed in this book (but not Scripture verses) are not, in all cases, exact quotations, as some have been edited for clarity and brevity. In all cases, the author has attempted to maintain the speaker's original intent. In some cases, quoted material for this book was obtained from secondary sources, primarily print media. While every effort was made to ensure the accuracy of these sources, the accuracy cannot be guaranteed. For additions, deletions, corrections, or clarifications in future editions of this text, please write Freeman-Smith.

Scripture quotations are taken from:

The Holy Bible, King James Version (KJV)

The Holy Bible, New International Version (NIV) Copyright © 1973, 1978, 1984, by International Bible Society. Used by permission of Zondervan Publishing House. All rights reserved.

The Holy Bible, New King James Version (NKJV) Copyright © 1982 by Thomas Nelson, Inc. Used by permission.

Holy Bible, New Living Translation, (NLT) copyright © 1996. Used by permission of Tyndale House Publishers, Inc., Wheaton, Illinois 60189. All rights reserved.

The Message (MSG)- This edition issued by contractual arrangement with NavPress, a division of The Navigators, U.S.A. Originally published by NavPress in English as THE MESSAGE: The Bible in Contemporary Language copyright 2002-2003 by Eugene Peterson. All rights reserved.

New Century Version®. (NCV) Copyright © 1987, 1988, 1991 by Word Publishing, a division of Thomas Nelson, Inc. All rights reserved. Used by permission.

The New American Standard Bible®, (NASB) Copyright © 1960, 1962, 1963, 1968, 1971, 1972, 1973, 1975, 1977, 1995 by The Lockman Foundation. Used by permission.

The Holman Christian Standard Bible™ (HCSB) Copyright © 1999, 2000, 2001 by Holman Bible Publishers. Used by permission.

Cover Design by Kim Russell / Wahoo Designs
Page Layout by Bart Dawson

ISBN 978-1-60587-355-8

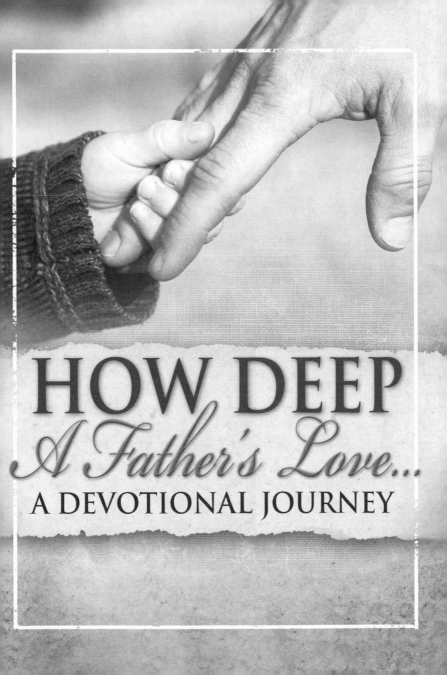

HOW DEEP
A Father's Love...
A DEVOTIONAL JOURNEY

Table of Contents

Introduction

Because you're reading this book, you probably answer to the name Dad, Daddy, Pop, Father, or some variation thereof. If so, congratulations: few of life's joys can match the glorious responsibility of leading your family in the will and the Word of God.

As a loving father, you are keenly aware of the priceless treasure that God has entrusted to your care; that treasure, of course, is your family. And as a Christian, you're also aware of another incalculable treasure that is yours for the asking: the gift of eternal life that was purchased by God's only begotten Son on the cross at Calvary. This devotional book serves as an inspirational reminder of these and other blessings that you, as a believer, can savor for a lifetime and beyond.

Every day provides opportunities to thank God for His gifts by putting Him where He belongs: at the center of your thoughts and prayers. When you do so, you will worship your Creator, not just with words, but also with deeds. And then, just as He promised, God will smile upon you, upon your children, and upon generations yet unborn.

A Father's Love

Now these three remain: faith, hope, and love. But the greatest of these is love.

1 Corinthians 13:13 HCSB

Few things in life are as precious or enduring as a father's love. Indeed, a father's love is powerful and priceless. The familiar words of 1st Corinthians 13 remind us that love is God's commandment. Faith is important, of course. So too is hope. But love is more important still.

Christ showed His love for us on the cross, and, as Christians, we are called upon to return Christ's love by sharing it. We are commanded (not advised, not encouraged . . . commanded!) to love one another just as Christ loved us (John 13:34). That's a tall order, but as believers, we are obligated to follow it. And as fathers, we are obligated to love our families just as our Heavenly Father first loved us.

More from God's Word

I pray that you, being rooted and firmly established in love, may be able to comprehend with all the saints what is the breadth and width, height and depth, and to know the Messiah's love that surpasses knowledge, so you may be filled with all the fullness of God.

Ephesians 3:17-19 HCSB

If I speak the languages of men and of angels, but do not have love, I am a sounding gong or a clanging cymbal.

1 Corinthians 13:1 HCSB

Dear friends, if God loved us in this way, we also must love one another.

1 John 4:11 HCSB

We love because He first loved us.

1 John 4:19 HCSB

Hatred stirs up conflicts, but love covers all offenses.

Proverbs 10:12 HCSB

More Ideas for Your Journey

No man truly has joy unless he lives in love.

Thomas Aquinas

Homes that are built on anything other than love are bound to crumble.

Billy Graham

To love another person is to see the face of God.

Victor Hugo

A Father's Prayer

Lord, You have given me the gift of love and You've asked me to share it. The gift of love is a precious gift indeed. Let me nurture love and treasure it. And, help me remember that the essence of love is not to receive it, but to give it, today and forever. Amen

Who's First?

You shall have no other gods before Me.

Exodus 20:3 NKJV

As you think about the nature of your relationship with God, remember this: you will always have some type of relationship with Him—it is inevitable that your life must be lived in relationship to God. The question is not if you will have a relationship with Him; the burning question is whether or not that relationship will be one that seeks to honor Him.

Are you willing to place God first in your life? And, are you willing to welcome God's Son into your heart? Unless you can honestly answer these questions with a resounding yes, then your relationship with God isn't what it could be or should be. Thankfully, God is always available, He's always ready to forgive, and He's waiting to hear from you now. The rest, of course, is up to you.

More from God's Word

Be careful not to forget the Lord.

Deuteronomy 6:12 HCSB

It is good to give thanks to the Lord, and to sing praises to Your name, O Most High; to declare Your lovingkindness in the morning, and Your faithfulness every night.

Psalm 92:1-2 NKJV

Love the Lord your God with all your heart, with all your soul, and with all your strength.

Deuteronomy 6:5 HCSB

The Devil said to Him, "I will give You their splendor and all this authority, because it has been given over to me, and I can give it to anyone I want. If You, then, will worship me, all will be Yours." And Jesus answered him, "It is written: You shall worship the Lord your God, and Him alone you shall serve."

Luke 4:6-8 HCSB

The thing you should want most is God's kingdom and doing what God wants. Then all these other things you need will be given to you.

Matthew 6:33 NCV

More Ideas for Your Journey

God is able to do anything He pleases with one ordinary person fully consecrated to Him.

Henry Blackaby and Claude King

We become whatever we are committed to.

Rick Warren

God calls us to be committed to Him, to be committed to making a difference, and to be committed to reconciliation.

Bill Hybels

A Father's Prayer

Dear Lord, today I will honor You with my thoughts, my actions, and my prayers. I will seek to please You, and I will strive to serve You. Your blessings are as limitless as Your love. And because I have been so richly blessed, I will worship You, Father, with thanksgiving in my heart and praise on my lips, this day and forever. Amen

Your Bright Future

What a God we have! And how fortunate we are to have him, this Father of our Master Jesus! Because Jesus was raised from the dead, we've been given a brand-new life and have everything to live for, including a future in heaven—and the future starts now!

1 Peter 1:3-4 MSG

How bright is your future? Well, if you're a faithful believer, God's plans for you are so bright that you'd better wear shades. But here's an important question: How bright do you believe your future to be? Are you expecting a terrific tomorrow, or are you dreading a terrible one? The answer you give will have a powerful impact on the way tomorrow turns out.

Do you trust in the ultimate goodness of God's plan for your life? Will you face tomorrow's challenges with optimism and hope? You should. After all, God created you for a very important reason: His reason. And you still have important work to do: His work.

Today, as you live in the present and look to the future, remember that God has an amazing plan for you. Act—and believe—accordingly.

More Ideas for Your Journey

Hoping for a good future without investing in today is like a farmer waiting for a crop without ever planting any seed.

John Maxwell

The pages of your past cannot be rewritten, but the pages of your tomorrows are blank.

Zig Ziglar

The Christian believes in a fabulous future.

Billy Graham

A Father's Prayer

Dear Lord, as I look to the future, I will place my trust in You. If I become discouraged, I will turn to You. If I am afraid, I will seek strength in You. You are my Father, and I will place my hope, my trust, and my faith in You. Amen

What Kind of Example?

You should be an example to the believers in speech, in conduct, in love, in faith, in purity.

1 Timothy 4:12 HCSB

Our children learn from the lessons we teach and the lives we live, but not necessarily in that order. As fathers, we serve as unforgettable role models for our children and our grandchildren. The lives we lead and the choices we make should serve as enduring examples of the spiritual abundance that is available to all who worship God and obey His commandments.

Are you God's obedient servant? Is your faith in Christ clearly demonstrated by the example that you set for your children? If so, you will be blessed by God, and so, of course, will they.

More from God's Word

You are the light that gives light to the world. In the same way, you should be a light for other people. Live so that they will see the good things you do and will praise your Father in heaven.

Matthew 5:14, 16 NCV

Set an example of good works yourself, with integrity and dignity in your teaching.

Titus 2:7 HCSB

Therefore since we also have such a large cloud of witnesses surrounding us, let us lay aside every weight and the sin that so easily ensnares us, and run with endurance the race that lies before us.

Hebrews 12:1 HCSB

In everything you do, stay away from complaining and arguing, so that no one can speak a word of blame against you. You are to live clean, innocent lives as children of God in a dark world full of crooked and perverse people. Let your lives shine brightly before them.

Philippians 2:14-15 NLT

More Ideas for Your Journey

We urgently need people who encourage and inspire us to move toward God and away from the world's enticing pleasures.

Jim Cymbala

A holy life will produce the deepest impression. Lighthouses blow no horns; they only shine.

D. L. Moody

In our faith we follow in someone's steps. In our faith we leave footprints to guide others. It's the principle of discipleship.

Max Lucado

A Father's Prayer

Lord, make me a worthy example to my family and friends. And, let my words and my deeds serve as a testimony to the changes You have made in my life. Let me praise You, Father, by following in the footsteps of Your Son, and let others see Him through me. Amen

Kindness Is a Choice

A kind man benefits himself, but a cruel man brings disaster on himself.

Proverbs 11:17 HCSB

Christ showed His love for us by willingly sacrificing His own life so that we might have eternal life: "But God demonstrates his own love for us in this: While we were still sinners, Christ died for us" (Romans 5:8 NIV). We, as Christ's followers, are challenged to share His love with kind words on our lips and praise in our hearts.

Just as Christ has been—and will always be—the ultimate friend to His flock, so should we be Christlike in the kindness and generosity that we show toward others, especially those who are most in need.

When we walk each day with Jesus—and obey the commandments found in God's Holy Word—we become worthy ambassadors for Christ. When we share the love of Christ, we share a priceless gift with the world. As His servants, we must do no less.

More from God's Word

Just as you want others to do for you, do the same for them.

Luke 6:31 HCSB

Finally, all of you be of one mind, having compassion for one another; love as brothers, be tenderhearted, be courteous.

1 Peter 3:8 NKJV

Love is patient; love is kind.

1 Corinthians 13:4 HCSB

And may the Lord make you increase and abound in love to one another and to all.

1 Thessalonians 3:12 NKJV

And be kind and compassionate to one another, forgiving one another, just as God also forgave you in Christ.

Ephesians 4:32 HCSB

More Ideas for Your Journey

Be so preoccupied with good will that you haven't room for ill will.

E. Stanley Jones

When you extend hospitality to others, you're not trying to impress people, you're trying to reflect God to them.

Max Lucado

Do all the good you can. By all the means you can. In all the ways you can. In all the places you can. At all the times you can. To all the people you can. As long as ever you can.

John Wesley

A Father's Prayer

Help me, Lord, to see the needs of those around me. Today, let me show courtesy to those who cross my path. Let me spread kind words in honor of Your Son. Today, let forgiveness rule my heart. And every day, Lord, let my love for Christ be demonstrated through the acts of kindness that I offer to those who need the healing touch of the Master's hand. Amen

A Life to Be Treasured

I have set before you life and death, blessing and curse. Choose life so that you and your descendants may live, love the Lord your God, obey Him, and remain faithful to Him. For He is your life, and He will prolong your life in the land the Lord swore to give to your fathers Abraham, Isaac, and Jacob.

Deuteronomy 30:19-20 HCSB

Life can be tough sometimes, but it's also wonderful—and it's a glorious gift from God. How will you use that gift? Will you treat this day as a precious treasure from your Heavenly Father, or will you take the next 24 hours for granted? The answer should be obvious: Every day, including this one, comes giftwrapped from God—your job is to unwrap that gift, to use it wisely, and to give thanks to the Giver.

Instead of sleepwalking through life, you must wake up and live in the precious present. Each waking moment holds the potential to celebrate, to serve, to share, or to love. Because you are a person with incalculable potential, each moment has incalculable value. Your challenge is to experience each day to the fullest as you seek to live in accordance with God's plan for your life. When you do, you'll experience His abundance and His peace.

Are you willing to treat this day (and every one hereafter) as a special gift to be savored and celebrated? You should—and if you seek to Live with a capital L, you most certainly will.

More from God's Word

He who follows righteousness and mercy finds life, righteousness and honor.

Proverbs 21:21 NKJV

I urge you now to live the life to which God called you.

Ephesians 4:1 NKJV

Shout triumphantly to the Lord, all the earth. Serve the Lord with gladness; come before Him with joyful songs.

Psalm 100:1-2 HCSB

Rejoice in the Lord always. Again I will say, rejoice!

Philippians 4:4 NKJV

More Ideas for Your Journey

You've heard the saying, "Life is what you make it." That means we have a choice. We can choose to have a life full of frustration and fear, but we can just as easily choose one of joy and contentment.

Dennis Swanberg

People, places, and things were never meant to give us life. God alone is the author of a fulfilling life.

Gary Smalley & John Trent

Life is a glorious opportunity.

Billy Graham

A Father's Prayer

Dear Lord, You have created this glorious universe, and You have created me. Let me live my life to the fullest, and let me use my life for Your glory, today and every day. Amen

God's Grace

But God, who is abundant in mercy, because of His great love that He had for us, made us alive with the Messiah even though we were dead in trespasses. By grace you are saved!

Ephesians 2:4-5 HCSB

Someone has said that GRACE stands for God's Redemption At Christ's Expense. It's true—God sent His Son so that we might be redeemed from our sins. In doing so, our Heavenly Father demonstrated His infinite mercy and His infinite love. We have received countless gifts from God, but none can compare with the gift of salvation. God's grace is the ultimate gift, and we owe Him the ultimate in thanksgiving.

The gift of eternal life is the priceless possession of everyone who accepts God's Son as Lord and Savior. We return our Savior's love by welcoming Him into our hearts and sharing His message and His love. When we do so, we are blessed not today and forever.

More from God's Word

My grace is sufficient for you, for My strength is made perfect in weakness.

2 Corinthians 12:9 NKJV

And we have seen and testify that the Father has sent the Son as Savior of the world.

1 John 4:14 NKJV

For by grace you are saved through faith, and this is not from yourselves; it is God's gift—not from works, so that no one can boast.

Ephesians 2:8-9 HCSB

In Him we have redemption through His blood, the forgiveness of our trespasses, according to the riches of His grace that He lavished on us with all wisdom and understanding.

Ephesians 1:7-8 HCSB

Therefore, since we are receiving a kingdom that cannot be shaken, let us hold on to grace. By it, we may serve God acceptably, with reverence and awe.

Hebrews 12:28 HCSB

More Ideas for Your Journey

The grace of God is sufficient for all our needs, for every problem, and for every difficulty, for every broken heart, and for every human sorrow.

Peter Marshall

You don't earn grace, and you don't deserve grace; you simply receive it as God's loving gift, and then share it with others.

Warren Wiersbe

The grace of God is infinite and eternal. As it had no beginning, so it can have no end, and being an attribute of God, it is as boundless as infinitude.

A. W. Tozer

A Father's Prayer

Lord, You have saved me by Your grace. Keep me mindful that Your grace is a gift that I can accept but cannot earn. I praise You for that priceless gift, today and forever. Let me share the good news of Your grace with a world that desperately needs Your healing touch. Amen

Doing the Right Thing

Lead a tranquil and quiet life in all godliness and dignity.

1 Timothy 2:2 HCSB

Oswald Chambers, the author of the Christian classic, *My Utmost for His Highest*, advised, "Never support an experience which does not have God as its source, and faith in God as its result." These words serve as a powerful reminder that, as Christians, we are called to walk with God and obey His commandments. But, we live in a world that presents countless temptations for adults and even more temptations for our children.

We Christians, when confronted with sin, have clear instructions: walk—or better yet run—in the opposite direction. When we do, we reap the blessings that God has promised to all those who live according to His will and His Word.

More from God's Word

Because the eyes of the Lord are on the righteous and His ears are open to their request. But the face of the Lord is against those who do evil.

1 Peter 3:12 HCSB

Flee from youthful passions, and pursue righteousness, faith, love, and peace, along with those who call on the Lord from a pure heart.

2 Timothy 2:22 HCSB

And now, Israel, what does the Lord your God ask of you except to fear the Lord your God by walking in all His ways, to love Him, and to worship the Lord your God with all your heart and all your soul?

Deuteronomy 10:12 HCSB

Do what is right and good in the Lord's sight, so that you may prosper and so that you may enter and possess the good land the Lord your God swore to [give] your fathers.

Deuteronomy 6:18 HCSB

More Ideas for Your Journey

The best evidence of our having the truth is our walking in the truth.

Matthew Henry

If we have the true love of God in our hearts, we will show it in our lives. We will not have to go up and down the earth proclaiming it. We will show it in everything we say or do.

D. L. Moody

The purity of motive determines the quality of action.

Oswald Chambers

A Father's Prayer

Holy Father, let my thoughts and my deeds be pleasing to You. I thank You, Lord, for Jesus, the One who took away my sins. Today and every day, I will follow in His footsteps so that my life can be a living testimony to Your love, to Your forgiveness, and to Your Son. Amen

Beyond Failure

Success, success to you, and success to those who help you, for your God will help you....

1 Chronicles 12:18 NIV

The occasional disappointments and failures of life are inevitable. Such setbacks are simply the price that we must occasionally pay for our willingness to take risks as we follow our dreams. But even when we encounter bitter disappointments, we must never lose faith.

As parents, we are far from perfect. And, without question, our children are imperfect as well. When we make mistakes, we must correct them and learn from them. And, when our children make mistakes, we must help them do likewise.

More Ideas for Your Journey

Do not be one of those who, rather than risk failure, never attempt anything.

Thomas Merton

Success or failure can be pretty well predicted by the degree to which the heart is fully in it.

John Eldredge

As long as a man keeps his faith in God and in himself nothing can permanently defeat him.

Wilferd Peterson

A Father's Prayer

Dear Lord, when I encounter failures and disappointments, keep me mindful that You are in control. Let me persevere—even if my soul is troubled—and let me follow Your Son, Jesus Christ, this day and forever. Amen

The Power of Patience

Be gentle to everyone, able to teach, and patient.

2 Timothy 2:23 HCSB

The rigors of parenting can test the patience of the most even-tempered dads. From time to time, even the most mannerly children may do things that worry us, or confuse us, or anger us. Why? Because they are children and because they are human. As loving parents, we must be patient with our children's shortcomings (just as they, too, must be patient with ours).

Sometimes, patience is the price we pay for being responsible fathers, and that's as it should be. After all, think how patient our Heavenly Father has been with us.

More from God's Word

Rejoice in hope; be patient in affliction; be persistent in prayer.

Romans 12:12 HCSB

Now we exhort you, brethren, warn those who are unruly, comfort the fainthearted, uphold the weak, be patient with all.

1 Thessalonians 5:14 NKJV

Love is patient; love is kind.

1 Corinthians 13:4 HCSB

A patient spirit is better than a proud spirit.

Ecclesiastes 7:8 HCSB

Therefore the Lord is waiting to show you mercy, and is rising up to show you compassion, for the Lord is a just God. Happy are all who wait patiently for Him.

Isaiah 30:18 HCSB

More Ideas for Your Journey

You can't step in front of God and not get in trouble. When He says, "Go three steps," don't go four.

Charles Stanley

In all negotiations of difficulties, a man may not look to sow and reap at once. He must prepare his business and so ripen it by degrees.

Francis Bacon

As we wait on God, He helps us use the winds of adversity to soar above our problems. As the Bible says, "Those who wait on the LORD . . . shall mount up with wings like eagles."

Billy Graham

A Father's Prayer

Heavenly Father, let me wait quietly for You. Let me live according to Your plan and according to Your timetable. When I am hurried, slow me down. When I become impatient with others, give me empathy. Today, I want to be a patient Christian, Dear Lord, as I trust in You and in Your master plan. Amen

A Willingness to Serve

Worship the Lord your God and . . . serve Him only.

Matthew 4:10 HCSB

Jesus teaches that the most esteemed men and women are not the leaders of society or the captains of industry. To the contrary, Jesus teaches that the greatest among us are those who choose to minister and to serve.

Today, you may feel the temptation to build yourself up in the eyes of your neighbors. Resist that temptation. Instead, serve your neighbors quietly and without fanfare. Find a need and fill it . . . humbly. Lend a helping hand and share a word of kindness . . . anonymously.

Today, take the time to minister to those in need. Then, when you have done your best to serve your neighbors and to serve your God, you can rest comfortably knowing that in the eyes of God you have achieved greatness. And God's eyes, after all, are the only ones that really count.

More from God's Word

A person should consider us in this way: as servants of Christ and managers of God's mysteries. In this regard, it is expected of managers that each one be found faithful.

1 Corinthians 4:1-2 HCSB

If they serve Him obediently, they will end their days in prosperity and their years in happiness.

Job 36:11 HCSB

We must do the works of Him who sent Me while it is day. Night is coming when no one can work.

John 9:4 HCSB

Serve the Lord with gladness.

Psalm 100:2 HCSB

If anyone serves Me, let him follow Me; and where I am, there My servant will be also. If anyone serves Me, him My Father will honor.

John 12:26 NKJV

More Ideas for Your Journey

In Jesus, the service of God and the service of the least of the brethren were one.

Dietrich Bonhoeffer

God does not do anything with us, only through us.

Oswald Chambers

Make it a rule, and pray to God to help you to keep it, never, if possible, to lie down at night without being able to say: "I have made one human being at least a little wiser, or a little happier, or at least a little better this day."

Charles Kingsley

A Father's Prayer

Dear Lord, when Jesus humbled Himself and became a servant, He also became an example for me. Make me a faithful steward of my gifts, and let me be a humble servant to my loved ones, to my friends, and to those in need. Amen

Discipline Now

But I discipline my body and bring it into subjection, lest, when I have preached to others, I myself should become disqualified.

1 Corinthians 9:27 NKJV

Are you a self-disciplined dad? If so, congratulations . . . if not, God wants to have a little talk with you.

You live in a world in which leisure is glorified and indifference is often glamorized. But God has other plans. He did not create you to be ordinary; He created you for far greater things.

Life's greatest rewards aren't likely to fall into your lap. To the contrary, your greatest accomplishments will probably require lots of work, which is perfectly fine with God. After all, He knows that you're up to the task, and He has big plans for you. God will do His part to fulfill those plans, and the rest, of course, is up to you.

Now, are you steadfast in your determination to be a self-disciplined man? If so, congratulations . . . if not, re-read this little essay—and keep reading it—until God's message finally sinks in.

More from God's Word

No discipline seems enjoyable at the time, but painful. Later on, however, it yields the fruit of peace and righteousness to those who have been trained by it.

Hebrews 12:11 HCSB

The one who follows instruction is on the path to life, but the one who rejects correction goes astray.

Proverbs 10:17 HCSB

For this very reason, make every effort to supplement your faith with goodness, goodness with knowledge, knowledge with self-control, self-control with endurance, endurance with godliness.

2 Peter 1:5-6 HCSB

So prepare your minds for service and have self-control.

1 Peter 1:13 NCV

God hasn't invited us into a disorderly, unkempt life but into something holy and beautiful—as beautiful on the inside as the outside.

1 Thessalonians 4:7 MSG

More Ideas for Your Journey

If one examines the secret behind a championship football team, a magnificent orchestra, or a successful business, the principal ingredient is invariably discipline.

James Dobson

Personal humility is a spiritual discipline and the hallmark of the service of Jesus.

Franklin Graham

The alternative to discipline is disaster.

Vance Havner

A Father's Prayer

Heavenly Father, make me a man of discipline and righteousness. Let me teach others by the faithfulness of my conduct, and let me follow Your will and Your Word, today and every day. Amen

Give Encouragement

But encourage each other daily, while it is still called today,
so that none of you is hardened by sin's deception.

Hebrews 3:13 HCSB

Every member of your family needs a regular supply of encouraging words and pats on the back. And you need the rewards that God gives to those enthusiastic dads who are a continual source of encouragement to their wives and children.

In his letter to the Ephesians, Paul writes, "Do not let any unwholesome talk come out of your mouths, but only what is helpful for building others up according to their needs, that it may benefit those who listen" (4:29 NIV). This passage reminds us that, as Christians, we are instructed to choose our words carefully so as to build others up through wholesome, honest encouragement. How can we build others up? By celebrating their victories and their accomplishments. As the old saying goes, "When someone does something good, applaud—you'll make two people happy."

Today, look for the good in others—starting with your family. And then, celebrate the good that you find.

When you do, you'll be a powerful force of encouragement in the world . . . and a worthy servant to your God.

More from God's Word

*Therefore encourage one another and build each other up as
you are already doing.*

1 Thessalonians 5:11 HCSB

*I want their hearts to be encouraged and joined together
in love, so that they may have all the riches of assured
understanding, and have the knowledge of God's mystery—
Christ.*

Colossians 2:2 HCSB

*Carry one another's burdens; in this way you will fulfill the
law of Christ.*

Galatians 6:2 HCSB

*And let us be concerned about one another in order to
promote love and good works.*

Hebrews 10:24 HCSB

More Ideas for Your Journey

The secret of success is to find a need and fill it, to find a hurt and heal it, to find somebody with a problem and offer to help solve it.

Robert Schuller

Do you wonder where you can go for encouragement and motivation? Run to Jesus.

Max Lucado

A lot of people have gone further than they thought they could because someone else thought they could.

Zig Ziglar

A Father's Prayer

Dear Lord, make me a man who is quick to celebrate the accomplishments of others. Make me a source of genuine, lasting encouragement to my family and friends. And let my words and deeds be worthy of Your Son, the One who gives me strength and salvation, this day and for all eternity. Amen

Saying "Thanks" to God

In everything give thanks; for this is the will of God in Christ Jesus for you.

1 Thessalonians 5:18 NKJV

The words of 1 Thessalonians 5:18 remind us to give thanks in every circumstance of life. But sometimes, when our hearts are troubled and our spirits are crushed, we don't feel like celebrating. Yet even when the clouds of despair darken our lives, God offers us His love, His strength, and His grace. And as believers, we must thank Him.

Have you thanked God today for blessings that are too numerous to count? Have you offered Him your heartfelt prayers and your wholehearted praise? If not, it's time slow down and to offer a prayer of thanksgiving to the One who has given you life on earth and life eternal.

No matter our circumstances, we owe God so much more than we can ever repay, and the least we can do is to thank Him.

More from God's Word

Thanks be to God for His indescribable gift.

2 Corinthians 9:15 HCSB

And let the peace of the Messiah, to which you were also called in one body, control your hearts. Be thankful.

Colossians 3:15 HCSB

It is good to give thanks to the Lord, and to sing praises to Your name, O Most High.

Psalm 92:1 NKJV

Enter into His gates with thanksgiving, and into His courts with praise. Be thankful to Him, and bless His name. For the Lord is good; His mercy is everlasting, and His truth endures to all generations.

Psalm 100:4-5 NKJV

And whatever you do, in word or in deed, do everything in the name of the Lord Jesus, giving thanks to God the Father through Him.

Colossians 3:17 HCSB

More Ideas for Your Journey

We ought to give thanks for all fortune: if it is good, because it is good, if bad, because it works in us patience, humility, and the contempt of this world along with the hope of our eternal country.

C. S. Lewis

The words "thank" and "think" come from the same root word. If we would think more, we would thank more.

Warren Wiersbe

It is only with gratitude that life becomes rich.

Dietrich Bonhoeffer

A Father's Prayer

Lord, You have blessed me with a loving family—make me a father who is thankful, loving, responsible, and wise. I praise You, Father, for the gift of Your Son and for the gift of salvation. Let me be a joyful Christian and a worthy example, this day and every day that I live. Amen

Devotion 15

Time for Silence

Be silent before the Lord and wait expectantly for Him.

Psalm 37:7 HCSB

Do you take time each day for an extended period of silence? And during those precious moments, do you sincerely open your heart to your Creator? If so, you are wise and you are blessed.

The world can be a noisy place, a place filled to the brim with distractions, interruptions, and frustrations. And if you're not careful, the struggles and stresses of everyday living can rob you of the peace that should rightfully be yours because of your personal relationship with Christ. So take time each day to quietly commune with your Savior. When you do, those moments of silence will enable you to participate more fully in the only source of peace that endures: God's peace.

More from God's Word

In quietness and confidence shall be your strength.

Isaiah 30:15 NKJV

The one who is from God listens to God's words. This is why you don't listen, because you are not from God.

John 8:47 HCSB

What's this? Fools out shopping for wisdom! They wouldn't recognize it if they saw it!

Proverbs 17:16 MSG

I wait quietly before God, for my hope is in him.

Psalm 62:5 NLT

Be still, and know that I am God.

Psalm 46:10 NKJV

More Ideas for Your Journey

If the pace and the push, the noise and the crowds are getting to you, it's time to stop the nonsense and find a place of solace to refresh your spirit.

Charles Swindoll

Silence is as fit a garment for devotion as any other language.

C. H. Spurgeon

Growth takes place in quietness, in hidden ways, in silence and solitude. The process is not accessible to observation.

Eugene Peterson

A Father's Prayer

Dear Lord, in the quiet moments of this day, I will turn my thoughts and prayers to You. In silence, I will sense Your presence, and I will seek Your will for my life, knowing that when I accept Your peace, I will be blessed today and throughout eternity. Amen

Tackling Tough Times

God is our refuge and strength, always ready to help in times of trouble. So we will not fear, even if earthquakes come and mountains crumble to the sea.

Psalm 46:1-2 NLT

Are you a dad who has endured tough times? If so, welcome to the club! From time to time, all of us face adversity, discouragement, or disappointment. When we do, God stands ready to protect us. Psalm 147 promises, "He heals the brokenhearted, and binds their wounds" (v. 3, NIV). When we are troubled, we must call upon God, and then, in His own time and according to His own plan, He will heal us.

Life is often challenging, but as Christians, we must not be afraid. God loves us, and He will protect us. In times of hardship, He will comfort us; in times of sorrow, He will dry our tears. When we are troubled, or weak, or sorrowful, God is always with us. We must build our lives on the rock that cannot be shaken...we must trust in God. Always.

More from God's Word

When you are in distress and all these things have happened to you, you will return to the Lord your God in later days and obey Him. He will not leave you, destroy you, or forget the covenant with your fathers that He swore to them by oath, because the Lord your God is a compassionate God.

Deuteronomy 4:30-31 HCSB

Whatever has been born of God conquers the world. This is the victory that has conquered the world: our faith.

1 John 5:4 HCSB

Dear friends, when the fiery ordeal arises among you to test you, don't be surprised by it, as if something unusual were happening to you. Instead, as you share in the sufferings of the Messiah rejoice, so that you may also rejoice with great joy at the revelation of His glory.

1 Peter 4:12-13 HCSB

We are pressured in every way but not crushed; we are perplexed but not in despair.

2 Corinthians 4:8 HCSB

More Ideas for Your Journey

Your greatest ministry will likely come out of your greatest hurt.

Rick Warren

God will not permit any troubles to come upon us unless He has a specific plan by which great blessing can come out of the difficulty.

Peter Marshall

Jesus does not say, "There is no storm." He says, I am here, do not toss, but trust."

Vance Havner

A Father's Prayer

Heavenly Father, You are my strength and my refuge. As I journey through this day, I know that I may encounter disappointments and losses. When I am troubled, let me turn to You. Keep me steady, Lord, and renew a right spirit inside of me this day and forever. Amen

Moving Mountains

I assure you: If anyone says to this mountain, "Be lifted up and thrown into the sea," and does not doubt in his heart, but believes that what he says will happen, it will be done for him.

Mark 11:23 HCSB

Because we live in a demanding world, all of us have mountains to climb and mountains to move. Moving those mountains requires faith.

Are you a mountain-moving guy whose faith is evident for all to see? Or, are you a spiritual underachiever? As you think about the answer to that question, consider this: God needs more people who are willing to move mountains for His glory and for His kingdom.

Every life—including yours—is a series of wins and losses. Every step of the way, through every triumph and tragedy, God walks with you, ready and willing to strengthen you. The next time you find your courage tested to the limit, remember to take your fears to God. If you call upon Him, you will be comforted. Whatever your challenge, whatever your trouble, rest assured God can handle it.

When you place your faith, your trust, indeed your life in the hands of your Heavenly Father, you'll be amazed at the marvelous things He can do with you and through you. So strengthen your faith through praise, through worship, through Bible study, and through prayer. And trust God's plans. With Him, all things are possible, and He stands ready to open a world of possibilities to you.

More from God's Word

If you do not stand firm in your faith, then you will not stand at all.

Isaiah 7:9 HCSB

Be alert, stand firm in the faith, be brave and strong.

1 Corinthians 16:13 HCSB

For we walk by faith, not by sight.

2 Corinthians 5:7 HCSB

Now faith is the reality of what is hoped for, the proof of what is not seen.

Hebrews 11:1 HCSB

More Ideas for Your Journey

Faith is confidence in the promises of God or confidence that God will do what He has promised.

Charles Stanley

I do not want merely to possess a faith; I want a faith that possesses me.

Charles Kingsley

Only God can move mountains, but faith and prayer can move God.

E. M. Bounds

A Father's Prayer

Dear Lord, I want faith that moves mountains. You have big plans for this world and big plans for me. Help me fulfill those plans, Father, as I follow in the footsteps of Your Son. Amen

The Search for Purpose

For it is God who is working among you both the willing and the working for His good purpose.

Philippians 2:13 HCSB

L ife is best lived on purpose. And purpose, like everything else in the universe, begins with God. Whether you realize it or not, God has a plan for your life, a divine calling, a direction in which He is leading you. When you welcome God into your heart and establish a genuine relationship with Him, He will begin, in time, to make His purposes known.

Sometimes, God's intentions will be clear to you; other times, God's plan will seem uncertain at best. But even on those difficult days when you are unsure which way to turn, you must never lose sight of these overriding facts: God created you for a reason; He has important work for you to do; and He's waiting patiently for you to do it.

And the next step is up to you.

More from God's Word

We know that all things work together for the good of those who love God: those who are called according to His purpose.

Romans 8:28 HCSB

I will instruct you and show you the way to go; with My eye on you, I will give counsel.

Psalm 32:8 HCSB

You reveal the path of life to me; in Your presence is abundant joy; in Your right hand are eternal pleasures.

Psalm 16:11 HCSB

Commit your activities to the Lord and your plans will be achieved.

Proverbs 16:3 HCSB

Whatever you do, do all to the glory of God.

1 Corinthians 10:31 NKJV

More Ideas for Your Journey

We must focus on prayer as the main thrust to accomplish God's will and purpose on earth. The forces against us have never been greater, and this is the only way we can release God's power to become victorious.

John Maxwell

When God speaks to you through the Bible, prayer, circumstances, the church, or in some other way, he has a purpose in mind for your life.

Henry Blackaby and Claude King

Oh Lord, let me not live to be useless.

John Wesley

A Father's Prayer

Dear Lord, let Your purposes be my purposes. Let Your priorities be my priorities. Let Your will be my will. Let Your Word be my guide. And, let me grow in faith and in wisdom today and every day. Amen

Need Strength?

Create in me a pure heart, O God, and renew a steadfast spirit within me. Do not cast me from your presence or take your Holy Spirit from me. Restore to me the joy of your salvation and grant me a willing spirit, to sustain me.

Psalm 51:10-12 NIV

God is a never-ending source of strength and courage if we call upon Him. When we are weary, He gives us strength. When we see no hope, God reminds us of His promises. When we grieve, God wipes away our tears.

Do you feel overwhelmed by today's responsibilities? Do you feel pressured by the ever-increasing demands of 21st-century life? Then turn your concerns and your prayers over to God. He knows your needs, and He has promised to meet those needs. Whatever your circumstances, God will protect you and care for you...if you let Him. Invite Him into your heart and allow Him to renew your spirit. When you trust Him and Him alone, He will never fail you.

More Ideas for Your Journey

Walking with God leads to receiving his intimate counsel, and counseling leads to deep restoration.

John Eldredge

One reason so much American Christianity is a mile wide and an inch deep is that Christians are simply tired. Sometimes you need to kick back and rest for Jesus' sake.

Dennis Swanberg

The resurrection of Jesus Christ is the power of God to change history and to change lives.

Bill Bright

A Father's Prayer

Dear Lord, sometimes the demands of the day leave me discouraged and frustrated. Renew my strength, Father, and give me patience and perspective. Today and every day, let me draw comfort and courage from Your promises, from Your love, and from Your Son. Amen

Choices

I am offering you life or death, blessings or curses. Now, choose life! . . . To choose life is to love the Lord your God, obey him, and stay close to him.

Deuteronomy 30:19-20 NCV

L ife is a series of decisions and choices. Each day, we make countless decisions that can bring us closer to God...or not. When we live according to God's commandments, we earn for ourselves the abundance and peace that He intends for our lives. But, when we turn our backs upon God by disobeying Him, we bring needless suffering upon ourselves and our families.

Do you seek spiritual abundance that can be yours through the person of God's only begotten Son? Then invite Christ into your heart and live according to His teachings. And, when you confront a difficult decision or a powerful temptation, seek God's wisdom and trust it. When you do, you will receive untold blessings—not only for this day, but also for all eternity.

More from God's Word

So I strive always to keep my conscience clear before God and man.

Acts 24:16 NIV

The thing you should want most is God's kingdom and doing what God wants. Then all these other things you need will be given to you.

Matthew 6:33 NCV

If you don't know what you're doing, pray to the Father. He loves to help. You'll get his help, and won't be condescended to when you ask for it. Ask boldly, believingly, without a second thought. People who "worry their prayers" are like wind-whipped waves. Don't think you're going to get anything from the Master that way, adrift at sea, keeping all your options open.

James 1:5-8 MSG

The wise people will shine like the brightness of the sky. Those who teach others to live right will shine like stars forever and ever.

Daniel 12:3 NCV

More Ideas for Your Journey

Life is a series of choices between the bad, the good, and the best. Everything depends on how we choose.

Vance Havner

Every day, I find countless opportunities to decide whether I will obey God and demonstrate my love for Him or try to please myself or the world system. God is waiting for my choices.

Bill Bright

We are either the masters or the victims of our attitudes. It is a matter of personal choice. Who we are today is the result of choices we made yesterday. Tomorrow, we will become what we choose today. To change means to choose to change.

John Maxwell

A Father's Prayer

Heavenly Father, I have many choices to make. Help me choose wisely as I follow in the footsteps of Your only begotten Son. Amen

Every Day with God

Morning by morning he wakens me and opens my understanding to his will. The Sovereign Lord has spoken to me, and I have listened.

Isaiah 50:4-5 NLT

Each new day is a gift from God, and if we are wise, we spend a few quiet moments each morning thanking the Giver. Daily life is woven together with the threads of habit, and no habit is more important to our spiritual health than the discipline of daily prayer and devotion to the Creator.

When we begin each day with our heads bowed and our hearts lifted, we remind ourselves of God's love, His protection, and His commandments. And if we are wise, we align our priorities for the coming day with the teachings and commandments that God has given us through His Holy Word.

Are you seeking to change some aspect of your life? Do you seek to improve the condition of your spiritual or physical health? If so, ask for God's help and ask for it many times each day . . . starting with your morning devotional.

More from God's Word

Teach me Your way, Lord, and I will live by Your truth. Give me an undivided mind to fear Your name.

Psalm 86:11 HCSB

I will instruct you and show you the way to go; with My eye on you, I will give counsel.

Psalm 32:8 HCSB

Happy is the man who finds wisdom, and the man who gains understanding.

Proverbs 3:13 NKJV

But grow in the grace and knowledge of our Lord and Savior Jesus Christ. To Him be the glory both now and to the day of eternity.

2 Peter 3:18 HCSB

In all your ways acknowledge Him, and He shall direct your paths.

Proverbs 3:6 NKJV

More Ideas for Your Journey

We must appropriate the tender mercy of God every day after conversion or problems quickly develop. We need his grace daily in order to live a righteous life.

Jim Cymbala

Wasted time of which we are later ashamed, temptations we yield to, weaknesses, lethargy in our work, disorder and lack of discipline in our thoughts and in our interaction with others—all these frequently have their root in neglecting prayer in the morning.

Dietrich Bonhoeffer

I suggest you discipline yourself to spend time daily in a systematic reading of God's Word. Make this "quiet time" a priority that nobody can change.

Warren Wiersbe

A Father's Prayer

Lord, help me to hear Your direction for my life in the quiet moments when I study Your Holy Word. And as I go about my daily activities, let everything that I say and do be pleasing to You. Amen

Beyond Materialism

> *Don't collect for yourselves treasures on earth, where moth and rust destroy and where thieves break in and steal. But collect for yourselves treasures in heaven, where neither moth nor rust destroys, and where thieves don't break in and steal. For where your treasure is, there your heart will be also.*
>
> Matthew 6:19-21 HCSB

I n our modern society, we need money to live. But as Christians, we must never make the acquisition of money the central focus of our lives. Money is a tool, but it should never overwhelm our sensibilities. The focus of life must be squarely on things spiritual, not things material.

Whenever we place our love for material possessions above our love for God—or when we yield to the countless other temptations of everyday living—we find ourselves engaged in a struggle between good and evil, a clash between God and Satan. Our responses to these struggles have implications that echo throughout our families and throughout our communities. Let us choose wisely by freeing ourselves from that subtle yet powerful temptation: the temptation to love the world more than we love God.

More from God's Word

And He told them, "Watch out and be on guard against all greed, because one's life is not in the abundance of his possessions."

Luke 12:15 HCSB

For what does it benefit a man to gain the whole world yet lose his life? What can a man give in exchange for his life?

Mark 8:36-37 HCSB

Anyone trusting in his riches will fall, but the righteous will flourish like foliage.

Proverbs 11:28 HCSB

For the mind-set of the flesh is death, but the mind-set of the Spirit is life and peace.

Romans 8:6 HCSB

More Ideas for Your Journey

When possessions become our god, we become materialistic and greedy . . . and we forfeit our contentment and our joy.

Charles Swindoll

He is no fool who gives what he cannot keep to gain what he cannot lose.

Jim Elliot

If you want to be truly happy, you won't find it on an endless quest for more stuff. You'll find it in receiving God generosity and then passing that generosity along.

Bill Hybels

A Father's Prayer

Lord, my greatest possession is my relationship with You through Jesus Christ. You have promised that when I first seek Your kingdom and Your righteousness, You will give me whatever I need. Let me trust You completely, Lord, for my needs, both material and spiritual, this day and always. Amen

Follow Him

"Follow Me," Jesus told them, "and I will make you into fishers of men!" Immediately they left their nets and followed Him.

Mark 1:17-18 HCSB

Whom will you walk with today? Will you walk with people who worship the ways of the world? Or will you walk with the Son of God?

Jesus walks with you. Are you walking with Him? Hopefully, you will choose to walk with Him today and every day of your life.

Jesus has called upon believers of every generation (and that includes you) to follow in His footsteps. And God's Word promises that when you follow in Christ's footsteps, you will learn how to live freely and lightly (Matthew 11:28-30).

Are you worried about the day ahead? Be confident in God's power. He will never desert you. Are you concerned about the future? Be courageous and call upon God. He will protect you. Are you confused? Listen to the quiet voice of your Heavenly Father. He is not a God of confusion. Talk with God; listen to Him; follow His commandments . . . and walk with His Son—starting now.

More from God's Word

But whoever keeps His word, truly in him the love of God is perfected. This is how we know we are in Him: the one who says he remains in Him should walk just as He walked.

1 John 2:5-6 HCSB

We encouraged, comforted, and implored each one of you to walk worthy of God, who calls you into His own kingdom and glory.

1 Thessalonians 2:12 HCSB

If we live by the Spirit, we must also follow the Spirit.

Galatians 5:25 HCSB

More Ideas for Your Journey

Our responsibility is to feed from Him, to stay close to Him, to follow Him—because sheep easily go astray—so that we eternally experience the protection and companionship of our Great Shepherd the Lord Jesus Christ.

Franklin Graham

Christ is like a river that is continually flowing. There are always fresh supplies of water coming from the fountain-head, so that a man may live by it and be supplied with water all his life. So Christ is an ever-flowing fountain; he is continually supplying his people, and the fountain is not spent. They who live upon Christ may have fresh supplies from him for all eternity; they may have an increase of blessedness that is new, and new still, and which never will come to an end.

Jonathan Edwards

A Father's Prayer

Dear Lord, You sent Jesus to save the world and to save me. I thank You for Jesus, and I will do my best to follow Him, today and forever. Amen

Devotion 24

Celebrate!

Rejoice in the Lord always. I will say it again: Rejoice!
Philippians 4:4 HCSB

Are you a dad who celebrates life? Hopefully you are! God has richly blessed you, and He wants you to rejoice in His gifts.

God fills each day to the brim with possibilities, and He challenges each of us to use our gifts for the glory of His kingdom. When we honor the Father and place Him at the center of our lives, every day becomes a cause for celebration.

Today is a non-renewable resource—once it's gone, it's gone forever. Our responsibility—both as fathers and as believers—is to use this day in the service of God's will and in the service of His people. When we do so, we enrich our own lives and the lives of those whom we love. And the Father smiles.

More from God's Word

This is the day the LORD has made; we will rejoice and be glad in it.

Psalm 118:24 NKJV

Delight yourself also in the Lord, and He shall give you the desires of your heart.

Psalm 37:4 NKJV

If they serve Him obediently, they will end their days in prosperity and their years in happiness.

Job 36:11 HCSB

The one who understands a matter finds success, and the one who trusts in the Lord will be happy.

Proverbs 16:20 HCSB

Rejoice in the Lord, you righteous ones; praise from the upright is beautiful.

Psalm 33:1 HCSB

More Ideas for Your Journey

Let God have you, and let God love you—and don't be surprised if your heart begins to hear music you've never heard and your feet learn to dance as never before.

Max Lucado

Some of us seem so anxious about avoiding hell that we forget to celebrate our journey toward heaven.

Philip Yancey

Joy is the great note all throughout the Bible.

Oswald Chambers

A Father's Prayer

Dear Lord, You have given me so many reasons to celebrate. Today, let me choose an attitude of cheerfulness. Let me be a joyful Christian, Lord, quick to laugh and slow to anger. Let me praise You, Lord, and give thanks for Your blessings. Today is Your creation; let me celebrate it…and You. Amen

Devotion 25

Getting the Work Done

Whatever your hands find to do, do with [all] your strength.

Ecclesiastes 9:10 HCSB

Providing for your family requires work and lots of it. And as a hardworking dad, you have earned the gratitude of your loved ones and the praise of your Heavenly Father.

It has been said that there are no shortcuts to any place worth going. Dads agree. Making the grade in today's competitive workplace is not easy. In fact, it can be very difficult indeed. But, even when the workday is long and the workload is difficult, we must not become discouraged.

God did not create us for lives of mediocrity; He created us for far greater things. Earning great things usually requires determination, persistence, and hard work—which is perfectly fine with God. After all, He knows that we're up to the task, and He has big plans for us. Very big plans...

More from God's Word

Do not be lazy but work hard, serving the Lord with all your heart.

Romans 12:11 NCV

He did it with all his heart. So he prospered.

2 Chronicles 31:21 NKJV

Don't work only while being watched, in order to please men, but as slaves of Christ, do God's will from your heart. Render service with a good attitude, as to the Lord and not to men.

Ephesians 6:6-7 HCSB

We must do the works of Him who sent Me while it is day. Night is coming when no one can work.

John 9:4 HCSB

In fact, when we were with you, this is what we commanded you: "If anyone isn't willing to work, he should not eat."

2 Thessalonians 3:10 HCSB

More Ideas for Your Journey

Chiefly the mold of a man's fortune is in his own hands.

Francis Bacon

People who work for money only are usually miserable, because there is no fulfillment and no meaning to what they do.

Dave Ramsey

If you want to reach your potential, you need to add a strong work ethic to your talent.

John Maxwell

A Father's Prayer

Lord, let me be an industrious worker in Your fields. Those fields are ripe, Lord, and Your workers are few. Let me be counted as Your faithful, diligent servant today, and every day. Amen

Devotion 26

Accepting Life

The Lord says, "Forget what happened before, and do not think about the past. Look at the new thing I am going to do. It is already happening. Don't you see it? I will make a road in the desert and rivers in the dry land."

Isaiah 43:18-19 NCV

Sometimes, we must accept life on its terms, not our own. Life has a way of unfolding, not as we will, but as it will. And sometimes, there is precious little we can do to change things.

When events transpire that are beyond our control, we have a choice: we can either learn the art of acceptance, or we can make ourselves miserable as we struggle to change the unchangeable.

We must entrust the things we cannot change to God. Once we have done so, we can prayerfully and faithfully tackle the important work that He has placed before us: doing something about the things we can change . . . and doing it sooner rather than later.

More from God's Word

A man's heart plans his way, but the Lord determines his steps.

Proverbs 16:9 HCSB

For everything created by God is good, and nothing should be rejected if it is received with thanksgiving.

1 Timothy 4:4 HCSB

Should we accept only good from God and not adversity?

Job 2:10 HCSB

Come to terms with God and be at peace; in this way good will come to you.

Job 22:21 HCSB

He is the Lord. He will do what He thinks is good.

1 Samuel 3:18 HCSB

More Ideas for Your Journey

What cannot be altered must be borne, not blamed.

Thomas Fuller

Prayer may not get us what we want, but it will teach us to want what we need.

Vance Havner

Trust the past to God's mercy, the present to God's love, and the future to God's providence.

St. Augustine

A Father's Prayer

Dear Lord, let me live in the present, not the past. Let me focus on my blessings, not my sorrows. Give me the wisdom to be thankful for the gifts that I do have, and not bitter about the things that I don't have. Let me accept what was, let me give thanks for what is, and let me have faith in what most surely will be: the promise of eternal life with You. Amen

Those Difficult Days

Be strong and courageous, and do the work. Don't be afraid or discouraged, for the Lord God, my God, is with you. He won't leave you or forsake you.

1 Chronicles 28:20 HCSB

Being a godly father in this difficult world is no easy task. Ours is a time of uncertainty and danger, a time when even the most courageous dads have legitimate cause for concern. But as believers we can live courageously, knowing that we have been saved by a loving Father and His only begotten Son.

Are you anxious? Take those anxieties to God. Are you troubled? Take your troubles to Him. Does the world seem to be trembling beneath your feet? Seek protection from the One who cannot be moved. The same God who created the universe will protect you if you ask Him…so ask Him. And then live courageously, knowing that even in these troubled times, God is always as near as your next breath.

More from God's Word

For God has not given us a spirit of fearfulness, but one of power, love, and sound judgment.

2 Timothy 1:7 HCSB

Be alert, stand firm in the faith, be brave and strong.

1 Corinthians 16:13 HCSB

Haven't I commanded you: be strong and courageous? Do not be afraid or discouraged, for the Lord your God is with you wherever you go.

Joshua 1:9 HCSB

But when Jesus heard it, He answered him, "Don't be afraid. Only believe."

Luke 8:50 HCSB

But He said to them, "Why are you fearful, you of little faith?" Then He got up and rebuked the winds and the sea. And there was a great calm.

Matthew 8:26 HCSB

More Ideas for Your Journey

Take courage. We walk in the wilderness today and in the Promised Land tomorrow.

D. L. Moody

Do not let Satan deceive you into being afraid of God's plans for your life.

R. A. Torrey

The fear of God is the death of every other fear.

C. H. Spurgeon

A Father's Prayer

Lord, at times, this world is a fearful place. I fear for my family and especially for my children. Yet, You have promised me that You are with me always. With You as my protector, I am not afraid. Today, Dear Lord, let me live courageously as I place my trust in You. Amen

Nourished by the Word

Heaven and earth will pass away, but My words will never pass away.

Matthew 24:35 HCSB

God's Word is unlike any other book. The Bible is a roadmap for life here on earth and for life eternal. As Christians, we are called upon to study God's Holy Word, to trust its promises, to follow its commandments, and to share its Good News with the world.

As believers, we must study the Bible and meditate upon its meaning for our lives. Otherwise, we deprive ourselves of a priceless gift from our Creator. God's Holy Word is, indeed, a transforming, life-changing, one-of-a-kind treasure. And, a passing acquaintance with the Good Book is insufficient for Christians who seek to obey God's Word and to understand His will. After all, neither man nor woman should live by bread alone . . .

More from God's Word

But the word of the Lord endures forever. And this is the word that was preached as the gospel to you.

1 Peter 1:25 HCSB

All Scripture is inspired by God and is profitable for teaching, for rebuking, for correcting, for training in righteousness, so that the man of God may be complete, equipped for every good work.

2 Timothy 3:16-17 HCSB

For the word of God is living and effective and sharper than any two-edged sword, penetrating as far as to divide soul, spirit, joints, and marrow; it is a judge of the ideas and thoughts of the heart.

Hebrews 4:12 HCSB

The one who is from God listens to God's words. This is why you don't listen, because you are not from God.

John 8:47 HCSB

Man shall not live by bread alone, but by every word that proceeds from the mouth of God.

Matthew 4:4 NKJV

More Ideas for Your Journey

Try to get saturated with the gospel.

C. H. Spurgeon

God gives us a compass and a Book of promises and principles—the Bible—and lets us make our decisions day by day as we sense the leading of His Spirit. This is how we grow.

Warren Wiersbe

Reading news without reading the Bible will inevitably lead to an unbalanced life, an anxious spirit, a worried and depressed soul.

Bill Bright

A Father's Prayer

Heavenly Father, Your Word is a light unto the world; I will study it and trust it, and share it. In all that I do, help me be a worthy witness for You as I share the Good News of Your perfect Son and Your perfect Word. Amen

God Can Handle It

Cast your burden on the Lord, and He will support you; He will never allow the righteous to be shaken.

Psalm 55:22 HCSB

It's a promise that is made over and over again in the Bible: Whatever "it" is, God can handle it.

Life isn't always easy. Far from it! Sometimes, life can be very, very difficult, indeed. But even when the storm clouds form overhead, even during our darkest moments, we're protected by a loving Heavenly Father.

When we're worried, God can reassure us; when we're sad, God can comfort us. When our hearts are broken, God is not just near; He is here. So we must lift our thoughts and prayers to Him. When we do, He will answer our prayers. Why? Because He is our Shepherd, and He has promised to protect us now and forever.

More from God's Word

Finally, my brethren, be strong in the Lord and in the power of His might. Put on the whole armor of God, that you may be able to stand against the wiles of the devil.

Ephesians 6:10-11 NKJV

The Lord your God in your midst, the Mighty One, will save; He will rejoice over you with gladness, He will quiet you with His love, He will rejoice over you with singing.

Zephaniah 3:17 NKJV

God is my shield, saving those whose hearts are true and right.

Psalm 7:10 NLT

And my God shall supply all your need according to His riches in glory by Christ Jesus.

Philippians 4:19 NKJV

The LORD is my strength and my song; he has become my victory. He is my God, and I will praise him.

Exodus 15:2 NLT

More Ideas for Your Journey

The next time you're disappointed, don't panic. Don't give up. Just be patient and let God remind you he's still in control.

Max Lucado

We do not understand the intricate pattern of the stars in their course, but we know that He Who created them does, and that just as surely as He guides them, He is charting a safe course for us.

Billy Graham

You may not know what you are going to do; you only know that God knows what He is going to do.

Oswald Chambers

A Father's Prayer

Dear Lord, You rule over our world, and I will allow You to rule over my heart. I will obey Your commandments, I will study Your Word, and I will seek Your will for my life, today and every day of my life. Amen

Devotion 30

A Priceless Treasure

When Jesus realized how much this mattered to them, he brought a child to his side. "Whoever accepts this child as if the child were me, accepts me," he said. "And whoever accepts me, accepts the One who sent me. You become great by accepting, not asserting. Your spirit, not your size, makes the difference."

Luke 9:47-48 MSG

We are aware that God has entrusted us with priceless treasures from above—our children. Every child is a glorious gift from the Father. And, with the Father's gift comes profound responsibilities. Thoughtful parents understand the critical importance of raising their children with love, with family, with discipline, and with God.

If you're lucky enough to be a father, give thanks to God for the gift of your child. Whether you're the father of a newborn or a seasoned granddad, remember this: your child—like every child—is a child of God. May you, as a responsible father, behave accordingly.

More from God's Word

Train up a child in the way he should go, and when he is old he will not depart from it.

Proverbs 22:6 NKJV

Love the Lord your God with all your heart, with all your soul, and with all your strength. These words that I am giving you today are to be in your heart. Repeat them to your children. Talk about them when you sit in your house and when you walk along the road, when you lie down and when you get up.

Deuteronomy 6:5-7 HCSB

I have no greater joy than this: to hear that my children are walking in the truth.

3 John 1:4 HCSB

Therefore you shall lay up these words of mine in your heart and in your soul . . . . You shall teach them to your children, speaking of them when you sit in your house, when you walk by the way, when you lie down, and when you rise up.

Deuteronomy 11:18-19 NKJV

More Ideas for Your Journey

A child's life ought to be a child's life, full of simplicity.

Oswald Chambers

Happy is the child who happens in upon his parent from time to time to see him on his knees, or going aside regularly, to keep times with the Lord.

Larry Christenson

We can either grace our children, or damn them with unrequited wounds which never seem to heal. Men, as fathers, you have such power.

R. Kent Hughes

A Father's Prayer

Thank You, Lord, for the priceless gift of my children. Because I am theirs and they are mine, I am blessed beyond words. Let me always be mindful of the profound responsibilities of parenthood, and let me raise my children to know You and to walk with You always. Amen

Considering the Cross

But as for me, I will never boast about anything except the cross of our Lord Jesus Christ, through whom the world has been crucified to me, and I to the world.

Galatians 6:14 HCSB

As we consider Christ's sacrifice on the cross, we should be profoundly humbled and profoundly grateful. And today, as we come to Christ in prayer, we should do so in a spirit of quiet, heartfelt devotion to the One who gave His life so that we might have life eternal.

He was the Son of God, but He wore a crown of thorns. He was the Savior of mankind, yet He was put to death the cross. He offered His healing touch to an unsaved world, and yet the same hands that had healed the sick and raised the dead were pierced with nails.

Christ humbled Himself on a cross—for you. He shed His blood—for you. He has offered to walk with you through this life and throughout all eternity. As you approach Him today in prayer, think about His sacrifice and His grace. And be humble.

More Ideas for Your Journey

No man understands the Scriptures unless he is acquainted with the cross.

Martin Luther

There is no detour to holiness. Jesus came to the resurrection through the cross, not around it.

Leighton Ford

Come and see the victories of the cross. Christ's wounds are thy healings. His agonies, thy repose. His death, thy life. His sufferings, they salvation.

Matthew Henry

A Father's Prayer

Dear Jesus, You are my Savior and my protector. You suffered on the cross for me, and I will give You honor and praise every day of my life. I will honor You with my words, my thoughts, and my prayers. And I will live according to Your commandments, so that through me, others might come to know Your perfect love. Amen

Time to Praise God

Therefore, through Him let us continually offer up to God a sacrifice of praise, that is, the fruit of our lips that confess His name.

Hebrews 13:15 HCSB

When is the best time to praise God? In church? Before dinner is served? When we tuck little children into bed? None of the above. The best time to praise God is all day, every day, to the greatest extent we can, with thanksgiving in our hearts.

Too many of us, even well-intentioned believers, tend to "compartmentalize" our waking hours into a few familiar categories: work, rest, play, family time, and worship. To do so is a mistake. Worship and praise should be woven into the fabric of everything we do; it should never be relegated to a weekly three-hour visit to church on Sunday morning.

Mrs. Charles E. Cowman, the author of the classic devotional text, *Streams in the Desert*, wrote, "Two wings are necessary to lift our souls toward God: prayer and praise. Prayer asks. Praise accepts the answer." Today, find a little more time to lift your concerns to God in prayer, and praise Him for all that He has done. He's listening . . . and He wants to hear from you.

More from God's Word

Praise the Lord, all nations! Glorify Him, all peoples! For great is His faithful love to us; the Lord's faithfulness endures forever. Hallelujah!

Psalm 117 HCSB

So that at the name of Jesus every knee should bow—of those who are in heaven and on earth and under the earth—and every tongue should confess that Jesus Christ is Lord, to the glory of God the Father.

Philippians 2:10-11 HCSB

Enter into his gates with thanksgiving, and into his courts with praise: be thankful unto him, and bless his name. For the LORD is good; his mercy is everlasting; and his truth endureth to all generations.

Psalm 100:4-5 KJV

More Ideas for Your Journey

Be not afraid of saying too much in the praises of God; all the danger is of saying too little.

Matthew Henry

Worship is an act which develops feelings for God, not a feeling for God which is expressed in an act of worship. When we obey the command to praise God in worship, our deep, essential need to be in relationship with God is nurtured.

Eugene Peterson

Praise opens the window of our hearts, preparing us to walk more closely with God. Prayer raises the window of our spirit, enabling us to listen more clearly to the Father.

Max Lucado

A Father's Prayer

Heavenly Father, I come to You today with hope in my heart and praise on my lips. Make me a faithful steward of the blessings You have entrusted to me. Let me follow in Christ's footsteps today and every day that I live. And let my words and deeds praise You now and forever. Amen

Ignoring Sin

For everyone who practices wicked things hates the light and avoids it, so that his deeds may not be exposed. But anyone who lives by the truth comes to the light, so that his works may be shown to be accomplished by God.

John 3:20–21 HCSB

If we deny our sins, we allow those sins to flourish. And if we allow sinful behaviors to become habits, we invite hardships into our own lives and into the lives of our loved ones. When we yield to the distractions and temptations of this troubled world, we suffer. But God has other intentions, and His plans for our lives do not include sin or denial.

When we allow ourselves to encounter God's presence, He will lead us away from temptation, away from confusion, and away from the self-deception. God is the champion of truth and the enemy of denial. May we see ourselves through His eyes and conduct ourselves accordingly.

More Ideas for Your Journey

Man prefers to believe what he prefers to be true.

Francis Bacon

What I like about experience is that it is such an honest thing. You may take any number of wrong turnings; but keep your eyes open and you will not be allowed to go very far before the warning signs appear. You may have deceived yourself, but experience is not trying to deceive you. The universe rings true wherever you fairly test it.

C. S. Lewis

There's none so blind as those who will not see.

Matthew Henry

A Father's Prayer

Dear Lord, when I displease You, I do injury to myself, to my family, and to my community. Because sin distances me from You, Lord, I will fear sin and I will avoid sinful places. The fear of sinning against You is a healthy fear, Father, because it can motivate me to accomplish Your will. Let a healthy fear of sin guide my path, today and every day of my life. Amen

Big Dreams

But as it is written: What no eye has seen and no ear has heard, and what has never come into a man's heart, is what God has prepared for those who love Him.

1 Corinthians 2:9 HCSB

Are you willing to entertain the possibility that God has big plans in store for you? Hopefully so. Yet sometimes, especially if you've recently experienced a life-altering disappointment, you may find it difficult to envision a brighter future for yourself and your family. If so, it's time to reconsider your own capabilities . . . and God's.

Your Heavenly Father created you with unique gifts and untapped talents; your job is to tap them. When you do, you'll begin to feel an increasing sense of confidence in yourself and in your future.

It takes courage to dream big dreams. You will discover that courage when you do three things: accept the past, trust God to handle the future, and make the most of the time He has given you today.

More from God's Word

Looking at them, Jesus said, "With men it is impossible, but not with God, because all things are possible with God."

Mark 10:27 HCSB

Now may the God of hope fill you with all joy and peace in believing, so that you may overflow with hope by the power of the Holy Spirit.

Romans 15:13 HCSB

Where there is no vision, the people perish....

Proverbs 29:18 KJV

Be of good courage, and he shall strengthen your heart, all ye that hope in the LORD.

Psalm 31:24 KJV

Live full lives, full in the fullness of God. God can do anything, you know—far more than you could ever imagine or guess or request in your wildest dreams! He does it not by pushing us around but by working within us, his Spirit deeply and gently within us.

Ephesians 3:19-20 MSG

More Ideas for Your Journey

To make your dream come true, you have to stay awake.

Dennis Swanberg

You cannot out-dream God.

John Eldredge

Set goals so big that unless God helps you, you will be a miserable failure.

Bill Bright

A Father's Prayer

Dear Lord, give me the courage to dream and the faithfulness to trust in Your perfect plan. When I am worried or weary, give me strength for today and hope for tomorrow. Keep me mindful of Your healing power, Your infinite love, and Your eternal salvation. Amen

Forgiveness Now

All bitterness, anger and wrath, insult and slander must be removed from you, along with all wickedness. And be kind and compassionate to one another, forgiving one another, just as God also forgave you in Christ.

Ephesians 4:31-32 HCSB

Even the most mild-mannered dads will, on occasion, have reason to become angry with the shortcomings of family members and friends. But wise dads are quick to forgive others, just as God has forgiven them.

Forgiveness is God's commandment, but oh how difficult a commandment it can be to follow. Being frail, fallible, imperfect human beings, we are quick to anger, quick to blame, slow to forgive, and even slower to forget. No matter. Forgiveness, no matter how difficult, is God's way, and it must be our way, too.

If, in your heart, you hold bitterness against even a single person, forgive. If there exists even one person, alive or dead, whom you have not forgiven, follow God's commandment and His will for your life: forgive. If you are embittered against yourself for some past mistake or shortcoming, forgive. Then, to the best of your abilities, forget. And move on. Hatred and bitterness and regret are not part of God's plan for your life. Forgiveness is.

More from God's Word

See to it that no one repays evil for evil to anyone, but always pursue what is good for one another and for all.

1 Thessalonians 5:15 HCSB

A person's insight gives him patience, and his virtue is to overlook an offense.

Proverbs 19:11 HCSB

And forgive us our sins, for we ourselves also forgive everyone in debt to us.

Luke 11:4 HCSB

And whenever you stand praying, if you have anything against anyone, forgive him, so that your Father in heaven may also forgive you your wrongdoing.

Mark 11:25 HCSB

More Ideas for Your Journey

There is always room for more loving forgiveness within our homes.

James Dobson

Learning how to forgive and forget is one of the secrets of a happy Christian life.

Warren Wiersbe

God's heart of mercy provides for us not only pardon from sin but also a daily provision of spiritual food to strengthen us.

Jim Cymbala

A Father's Prayer

Lord, I know that I need to forgive others just as You have forgiven me. Help me to be an example of forgiveness to my children. Keep me mindful, Father, that I am never fully liberated until I have been freed from the chains of bitterness—and that You offer me that freedom through Your Son, Christ Jesus. Amen

Optimism Now

My cup runs over. Surely goodness and mercy shall follow me all the days of my life; and I will dwell in the house of the Lord Forever.

Psalm 23:5-6 NKJV

The words of Psalm 118:24 remind us of a profound yet simple truth: "This is the day which the LORD hath made; we will rejoice and be glad in it" (KJV).

As each day unfolds, we are literally surrounded by more opportunities than we can count—opportunities to improve our own lives and the lives of those we love. God's Word promises that each of us possesses the ability to experience earthly peace and spiritual abundance.

So, as we face the inevitable challenges of life here on earth, we must not become discouraged. We must, instead, arm ourselves with the promises of God and when we do, we can expect the very best that life—and God—has to offer.

More from God's Word

Make me hear joy and gladness.

Psalm 51:8 NKJV

But if we hope for what we do not see, we eagerly wait for it with patience.

Romans 8:25 HCSB

For God has not given us a spirit of fearfulness, but one of power, love, and sound judgment.

2 Timothy 1:7 HCSB

I am able to do all things through Him who strengthens me.

Philippians 4:13 HCSB

The Lord is my light and my salvation; whom shall I fear? The Lord is the strength of my life; of whom shall I be afraid?

Psalm 27:1 KJV

More Ideas for Your Journey

The popular idea of faith is of a certain obstinate optimism: the hope, tenaciously held in the face of trouble, that the universe is fundamentally friendly and things may get better.

J. I. Packer

Christ can put a spring in your step and a thrill in your heart. Optimism and cheerfulness are products of knowing Christ.

Billy Graham

A Father's Prayer

Lord, You care for me, You love me, and You have given me the priceless gift of eternal life through Your Son Jesus. Because of You, Lord, I have every reason to live each day with celebration and hope. Help me to face this day with a spirit of optimism and thanksgiving so that I may lift the spirits of those I meet as I share the Good News of Your Son. And, let me focus my thoughts on You and Your incomparable gifts today and forever. Amen

Discipline Has Rewards

Discipline yourself for the purpose of godliness.

1 Timothy 4:7 NASB

W ise fathers teach their children the importance of discipline using both words and examples. Disciplined dads understand that God doesn't reward laziness or misbehavior. To the contrary, God expects His believers to lead lives that are above reproach. And, He punishes those who disobey His commandments.

In Proverbs 28:19, God's message is clear: "He who works his land will have abundant food, but the one who chases fantasies will have his fill of poverty" (NIV). When we work diligently and consistently, we can expect a bountiful harvest. But we must never expect the harvest to precede the labor. First, we must lead lives of discipline and obedience; then, we will reap the never-ending rewards that God has promised.

More Ideas for Your Journey

Work is doing it. Discipline is doing it every day. Diligence is doing it well every day.

Dave Ramsey

As we seek to become disciples of Jesus Christ, we should never forget that the word disciple is directly related to the word discipline. To be a disciple of the Lord Jesus Christ is to know his discipline.

Dennis Swanberg

Discipline is training that develops and corrects.

Charles Stanley

A Father's Prayer

Lord, let me be a disciplined parent, and let me teach my children to lead disciplined lives. Let me be Your faithful servant, Lord, and let me teach faithfulness by my conduct and by my communications. Let me raise my family in the knowledge of Your Word, and let me follow Your commandments just as surely as I teach my children to obey You and to love You. Amen

Your Faith

Whoever serves me must follow me. Then my servant will be with me everywhere I am. My Father will honor anyone who serves me.

John 12:26 NCV

Are you a father whose faith is evident for all to see? Or are you a spiritual shrinking violet? God needs more men who are willing to stand up and be counted for Him.

Genuine faith is never meant to be locked up in the heart of a believer; to the contrary, it is meant to be shared. A man who wishes to share God's Good News with the world should begin by sharing that message with his own family.

Every life—including yours—is a series of successes and failures, celebrations and disappointments, joys and sorrows. Every step of the way, through every triumph and tragedy, God will stand by your side and strengthen you . . . if you have faith in Him. Jesus taught His disciples that if they had faith, they could move mountains. You can too, and so can your family . . . if you have faith.

More Ideas for Your Journey

A disciple is a follower of Christ. That means you take on His priorities as your own. His agenda becomes your agenda. His mission becomes your mission.

Charles Stanley

The heaviest end of the cross lies ever on His shoulders. If He bids us carry a burden, He carries it also.

C. H. Spurgeon

The essence of the Christian life is Jesus: that in all things He might have the preeminence, not that in some things He might have a place.

Franklin Graham

A Father's Prayer

Dear Jesus, because I am Your disciple, I will trust You, I will obey Your teachings, and I will share Your Good News. You have given me life abundant and life eternal, and I will follow You today and forever. Amen

Real Joy

I have spoken these things to you so that My joy may be in you and your joy may be complete.

John 15:11 HCSB

A re you a dad whose joy is evident for all to see? If so, congratulations: you're doing God's will. Psalm 100 reminds us that, as believers, we have every reason to celebrate: "Shout for joy to the LORD, all the earth. Worship the LORD with gladness" (vv. 1-2 NIV). Yet sometimes, amid the inevitable hustle and bustle of life here on earth, we can forfeit—albeit temporarily—the joy that God intends for our lives.

If you find yourself feeling discouraged or worse, it's time to slow down and have a quiet conversation with your Creator. If your heart is heavy, open the door of your soul to the Father and to His only begotten Son. Christ offers you His peace and His joy. Accept it and share it freely, just as Christ has freely shared His joy with you.

More from God's Word

Rejoice in the Lord always. I will say it again: Rejoice!

Philippians 4:4 HCSB

Delight yourself also in the Lord, and He shall give you the desires of your heart.

Psalm 37:4 NKJV

Make me hear joy and gladness.

Psalm 51:8 NKJV

Weeping may spend the night, but there is joy in the morning.

Psalms 30:5 HCSB

The Lord reigns; let the earth rejoice.

Psalm 97:1 NKJV

More Ideas for Your Journey

Joy comes from knowing God loves me and knows who I am and where I'm going . . . that my future is secure as I rest in Him.

James Dobson

When I met Christ, I felt that I had swallowed sunshine.

E. Stanley Jones

I choose joy. I will refuse the temptation to be cynical; cynicism is the tool of a lazy thinker. I will refuse to see people as anything less than human beings, created by God. I will refuse to see any problem as anything less than an opportunity to see God.

Max Lucado

A Father's Prayer

Dear Lord, You have blessed me with a loving family; make me thankful, loving, responsible, and wise. I praise You, Father, for the gift of Your Son and for the gift of salvation. Let me be a joyful Christian and a worthy example, this day and every day that I live. Amen

Powerful Perseverance

For you need endurance, so that after you have done God's will, you may receive what was promised.

Hebrews 10:36 HCSB

The occasional disappointments and failures of life are inevitable. Such setbacks are simply the price that we must pay for our willingness to take risks as we follow our dreams. But even when we encounter setbacks, we must never lose faith.

The reassuring words of Hebrews 10:36 serve as a comforting reminder that perseverance indeed pays: "You have need of endurance, so that when you have done the will of God, you may receive what was promised" (NASB).

Are you willing to trust God's Word? And are you willing to keep "fighting the good fight," even when you've experienced unexpected difficulties? If so, you may soon be surprised at the creative ways that God finds to help determined people like you . . . people who possess the wisdom and the courage to persevere.

More from God's Word

Do you not know that the runners in a stadium all race, but only one receives the prize? Run in such a way that you may win. Now everyone who competes exercises self-control in everything. However, they do it to receive a perishable crown, but we an imperishable one.

1 Corinthians 9:24-25 HCSB

But as for you, be strong; don't be discouraged, for your work has a reward.

2 Chronicles 15:7 HCSB

I have fought the good fight, I have finished the race, I have kept the faith.

2 Timothy 4:7 HCSB

So we must not get tired of doing good, for we will reap at the proper time if we don't give up.

Galatians 6:9 HCSB

Let us lay aside every weight and the sin that so easily ensnares us, and run with endurance the race that lies before us, keeping our eyes on Jesus, the source and perfecter of our faith.

Hebrews 12:1-2 HCSB

More Ideas for Your Journey

Jesus taught that perseverance is the essential element in prayer.

E. M. Bounds

Perseverance is more than endurance. It is endurance combined with absolute assurance and certainty that what we are looking for is going to happen.

Oswald Chambers

Battles are won in the trenches, in the grit and grime of courageous determination; they are won day by day in the arena of life.

Charles Swindoll

A Father's Prayer

Lord, when life is difficult, I am tempted to abandon hope in the future. But You are my God, and I can draw strength from You. Let me trust You, Father, in good times and in bad times. Let me persevere—even if my soul is troubled—and let me follow Your Son Jesus Christ this day and forever. Amen

Beyond Anger

But now you must also put away all the following: anger, wrath, malice, slander, and filthy language from your mouth.

Colossians 3:8 HCSB

The frustrations of everyday living can sometimes get the better of us, and we allow minor disappointments to cause us major problems. When we allow ourselves to become overly irritated by the inevitable ups and downs of life, and we become over-stressed, overheated, overanxious, and just plain angry.

When you allow yourself to become angry, you are certain to defeat at least one person: yourself. When you allow the minor frustrations of everyday life to hijack your emotions, you do harm to yourself and to your loved ones. So today and every day, guard yourself against the kind of angry thinking that inevitably takes a toll on your emotions and your relationships.

As the old saying goes, "Anger usually improves nothing but the arch of a cat's back." So don't allow feelings of anger or frustration to rule your life, or, for that matter, your day—your life is simply too short for that, and you deserve much better treatment than that . . . from yourself.

More from God's Word

Don't let your spirit rush to be angry, for anger abides in the heart of fools.

Ecclesiastes 7:9 HCSB

All bitterness, anger and wrath, insult and slander must be removed from you, along with all wickedness. And be kind and compassionate to one another, forgiving one another, just as God also forgave you in Christ.

Ephesians 4:31-32 HCSB

Everyone must be quick to hear, slow to speak, and slow to anger, for man's anger does not accomplish God's righteousness.

James 1:19-20 HCSB

A patient person [shows] great understanding, but a quick-tempered one promotes foolishness.

Proverbs 14:29 HCSB

More Ideas for Your Journey

Anger is the noise of the soul; the unseen irritant of the heart; the relentless invader of silence.

Max Lucado

Is there somebody who's always getting your goat? Talk to the Shepherd.

Anonymous

When you strike out in anger, you may miss the other person, but you will always hit yourself.

Jim Gallery

A Father's Prayer

Lord, sometimes, it is so easy to lose my temper and my perspective. When anger burdens my soul, enable me to calm myself and to be a witness to Your truth and righteousness. Let my children see me as a model of kindness and forgiveness, today and every day. Amen

Too Busy to Pray?

The intense prayer of the righteous is very powerful.

James 5:16 HCSB

Does your family pray together often, or just at church? Are you a little band of prayer warriors, or have you retreated from God's battlefield? Do you and yours pray only at mealtimes, or do you pray much more often than that? The answer to these questions will determine, to a surprising extent, the level of your family's spiritual health.

Jesus made it clear to His disciples: they should pray always. And so should you. Genuine, heartfelt prayer changes things and it changes you. When you lift your heart to the Father, you open yourself to a never-ending source of divine wisdom and infinite love.

Your family's prayers are powerful. So, as you go about your daily activities, remember God's instructions: "Rejoice always! Pray constantly. Give thanks in everything, for this is God's will for you in Christ Jesus" (1 Thessalonians 5:16-18 HCSB). Start praying in the morning and keep praying until you fall off to sleep at night. And rest assured: God is always listening, and He always wants to hear from you and your family.

More from God's Word

Let the words of my mouth and the meditation of my heart be acceptable in Your sight, O Lord, my strength and my Redeemer.

Psalm 19:14 NKJV

Yet He often withdrew to deserted places and prayed.

Luke 5:16 HCSB

Don't worry about anything, but in everything, through prayer and petition with thanksgiving, let your requests be made known to God.

Philippians 4:6 HCSB

Ask, and it shall be given you; seek, and ye shall find; knock, and it shall be opened unto you: for every one that asketh receiveth; and he that seeketh findeth; and to him that knocketh it shall be opened.

Matthew 7:7-8 KJV

More Ideas for Your Journey

Prayer connects us with God's limitless potential.

Henry Blackaby

God wants to remind us that nothing on earth or in hell can ultimately stand against the man or the woman who calls on the name of the Lord!

Jim Cymbala

God shapes the world by prayer. The more praying there is in the world, the better the world will be, and the mightier will be the forces against evil.

E. M. Bounds

A Father's Prayer

Dear Lord, I will open my heart to You. I will take my concerns, my fears, my plans, and my hopes to You in prayer. And, then, I will trust the answers that You give. You are my loving Father, and I will accept Your will for my life today and every day that I live. Amen

Beyond Fear

I sought the Lord, and He answered me and delivered me from all my fears.

Psalm 34:4 HCSB

We live in a world that is, at times, a frightening place. We live in a world that is, at times, a discouraging place. We live in a world where life-changing losses can be so painful and so profound that it seems we will never recover. But, with God's help, and with the help of encouraging family members and friends, we can recover.

During the darker days of life, we are wise to remember the words of Jesus, who reassured His disciples, saying, "Take courage! It is I. Don't be afraid" (Matthew 14:27 NIV). Then, with God's comfort and His love in our hearts, we can offer encouragement to others. And by helping them face their fears, we can, in turn, tackle our own problems with courage, determination, and faith.

More from God's Word

Even when I go through the darkest valley, I fear [no] danger, for You are with me.

Psalm 23:4 HCSB

Don't be afraid. Only believe.

Mark 5:36 HCSB

For I, the Lord your God, hold your right hand and say to you: Do not fear, I will help you.

Isaiah 41:13 HCSB

I sought the Lord, and He heard me, and delivered me from all my fears.

Psalm 34:4 NKJV

Do not fear, for I am with you; do not be afraid, for I am your God. I will strengthen you; I will help you; I will hold on to you with My righteous right hand.

Isaiah 41:10 HCSB

More Ideas for Your Journey

When we meditate on God and remember the promises He has given us in His Word, our faith grows, and our fears dissolve.

Charles Stanley

The Lord Jesus by His Holy Spirit is with me, and the knowledge of His presence dispels the darkness and allays any fears.

Bill Bright

One of the main missions of God is to free us from the debilitating bonds of fear and anxiety. God's heart is broken when He sees us so demoralized and weighed down by fear.

Bill Hybels

A Father's Prayer

Your Word reminds me, Lord, that even when I walk through the valley of the shadow of death, I need fear no evil, for You are with me, and You comfort me. Thank You, Lord, for a perfect love that casts out fear. Let me live courageously and faithfully this day and every day. Amen

Lifetime Learning

Start with God—the first step in learning is bowing down to God.

Proverbs 1:7 MSG

Whether you're twenty-two or a hundred and two, you've still got lots to learn. Even if you're a very wise man, God isn't finished with you yet, and He isn't finished teaching you important lessons about life here on earth and life eternal.

Do you seek to live a life of righteousness and wisdom? If so, you must continue to study the ultimate source of wisdom: the Word of God. You must associate, day in and day out, with godly men and women. And, you must act in accordance with your beliefs. When you study God's Word and live according to His commandments, you will become wise . . . and you will be a blessing to your friends, to your family, and to the world.

More from God's Word

The wisdom that is from above is first pure, then peaceable, gentle, and easy to be entreated, full of mercy and good fruits, without partiality, and without hypocrisy.

James 3:17 KJV

Reverence for the Lord is the foundation of true wisdom. The rewards of wisdom come to all who obey him.

Psalm 111:10 NLT

Do not deceive yourselves. If any one of you thinks he is wise by the standards of this age, he should become a "fool" so that he may become wise. For the wisdom of this world is foolishness in God's sight.

1 Corinthians 3:18-19 NIV

It is not good to have zeal without knowledge, nor to be hasty and miss the way.

Proverbs 19:2 NIV

Now if any of you lacks wisdom, he should ask God, who gives to all generously and without criticizing, and it will be given to him.

James 1:5 HCSB

More Ideas for Your Journey

The wonderful thing about God's schoolroom is that we get to grade our own papers. You see, He doesn't test us so He can learn how well we're doing. He tests us so we can discover how well we're doing.

Charles Swindoll

Today is yesterday's pupil.

Thomas Fuller

The wise man gives proper appreciation in his life to his past. He learns to sift the sawdust of heritage in order to find the nuggets that make the current moment have any meaning.

Grady Nutt

A Father's Prayer

Dear Lord, I have so much to learn. Help me to watch, to listen, to think, and to learn, every day of my life. Amen

Problem-solving 101

People who do what is right may have many problems, but the Lord will solve them all.

Psalm 34:19 NCV

L ife is an adventure in problem-solving. The question is not whether we will encounter problems; the real question is how we will choose to address them. When it comes to solving the problems of everyday living, we often know precisely what needs to be done, but we may be slow in doing it—especially if what needs to be done is difficult. So we put off till tomorrow what should be done today.

As a man living here in the 21st-century, you have your own set of challenges. As you face those challenges, you may be comforted by this fact: Trouble, of every kind, is temporary. Yet God's grace is eternal. And worries, of every kind, are temporary. But God's love is everlasting. The troubles that concern you will pass. God remains. And for every problem, God has a solution.

The words of Psalm 34 remind us that the Lord solves problems for "people who do what is right." And usually, doing "what is right" means doing the uncomfortable work of confronting our problems sooner rather than later. So with no further ado, let the problem-solving begin . . . right now.

More Ideas for Your Journey

We are all faced with a series of great opportunities, brilliantly disguised as unsolvable problems. Unsolvable without God's wisdom, that is.

Charles Swindoll

Life will be made or broken at the place where we meet and deal with obstacles.

E. Stanley Jones

Each problem is a God-appointed instructor.

Charles Swindoll

A Father's Prayer

Lord, sometimes my problems are simply too big for me, but they are never too big for You. Let me turn my troubles over to You, Lord, and let me trust in You today and for all eternity. Amen

Critics Beware

Don't criticize one another, brothers. He who criticizes a brother or judges his brother criticizes the law and judges the law. But if you judge the law, you are not a doer of the law but a judge.

James 4:11 HCSB

From experience, we know that it is easier to criticize than to correct; we understand that it is easier to find faults than solutions; and we realize that excessive criticism is usually destructive, not productive. Yet the urge to criticize others remains a powerful temptation for most of us. Our task, as obedient believers, is to break the twin habits of negative thinking and critical speech.

Negativity is highly contagious: we give it to others who, in turn, give it back to us. This cycle can be broken by positive thoughts, heartfelt prayers, and encouraging words. As thoughtful servants of a loving God, we can use the transforming power of Christ's love to break the chains of negativity. And we should.

More Ideas for Your Journey

The scrutiny we give other people should be for ourselves.

Oswald Chambers

We shall never come to the perfect man til we come to the perfect world.

Matthew Henry

Being critical of others, including God, is one way we try to avoid facing and judging our own sins.

Warren Wiersbe

A Father's Prayer

Help me, Lord, rise above the need to criticize others. May my own shortcomings humble me, and may I always be a source of genuine encouragement to my family and friends. Amen

Your Beliefs

Do what God's teaching says; when you only listen and do nothing, you are fooling yourselves.

James 1:22 NCV

In describing one's beliefs, actions are far better descriptors than words. Yet far too many of us spend more energy talking about our beliefs than living by them—with predictable consequences.

Is your life a picture book of your creed? Are your actions congruent with your beliefs? Are you willing to practice the philosophy that you preach?

Today and every day, make certain that your actions are guided by God's Word and by the conscience that He has placed in your heart. Don't treat your faith as if it were separate from your everyday life. Weave your beliefs into the very fabric of your day. When you do, God will honor your good works, and your good works will honor God.

More from God's Word

Everyone who believes that Jesus is the Messiah has been born of God, and everyone who loves the parent also loves his child.

1 John 5:1 HCSB

I know whom I have believed and am persuaded that He is able to guard what has been entrusted to me until that day.

2 Timothy 1:12 HCSB

Then He said to Thomas, "Put your finger here and observe My hands. Reach out your hand and put it into My side. Don't be an unbeliever, but a believer."

John 20:27 HCSB

Then Jesus told the centurion, "Go. As you have believed, let it be done for you." And his servant was cured that very moment.

Matthew 8:13 HCSB

All things are possible to him that believeth.

Mark 9:23 KJV

More Ideas for Your Journey

Once you have thoroughly examined your values and articulated them, you will be able to steer your life by them.

John Maxwell

Believe and do what God says. The life-changing consequences will be limitless, and the results will be confidence and peace of mind.

Franklin Graham

God calls us to be committed to Him, to be committed to making a difference, and to be committed to reconciliation.

Bill Hybels

A Father's Prayer

Heavenly Father, I believe in You, and I believe in Your Word. Help me to live in such a way that my actions validate my beliefs—and let the glory be Yours forever. Amen

The Right Kind of Fear

The fear of the Lord is the beginning of knowledge, but fools despise wisdom and instruction.

Proverbs 1:7 NKJV

God's hand shapes the universe, and it shapes our lives. God maintains absolute sovereignty over His creation, and His power is beyond comprehension. As believers, we must cultivate a sincere respect for God's awesome power. God has dominion over all things, and until we acknowledge His sovereignty, we lack the humility we need to live righteously, and we lack the humility we need to become wise.

The fear of the Lord is, indeed, the beginning of knowledge. So today, as you face the realities of everyday life, remember this: until you acquire a healthy, respectful fear of God's power, your education is incomplete, and so is your faith.

More from God's Word

To fear the Lord is to hate evil.

Proverbs 8:13 HCSB

The fear of the Lord is the beginning of wisdom, and the knowledge of the Holy One is understanding.

Proverbs 9:10 HCSB

The fear of the Lord is the beginning of wisdom; all who follow His instructions have good insight.

Psalm 111:10 HCSB

The fear of the Lord is a fountain of life, turning people from the snares of death.

Proverbs 14:27 HCSB

Don't consider yourself to be wise; fear the Lord and turn away from evil.

Proverbs 3:7 HCSB

More Ideas for Your Journey

The remarkable thing about fearing God is that when you fear God, you fear nothing else, whereas if you do not fear God, you fear everything else.

Oswald Chambers

When true believers are awed by the greatness of God and by the privilege of becoming His children, then they become sincerely motivated, effective evangelists.

Bill Hybels

A healthy fear of God will do much to deter us from sin.

Charles Swindoll

A Father's Prayer

Lord, You love me and protect me. I praise You, Father, for Your grace, and I respect You for Your infinite power. Let my greatest fear in life be the fear of displeasing You. Amen

Enthused About Life

Whatever you do, do it enthusiastically, as something done for the Lord and not for men.

Colossians 3:23 HCSB

D o you see each day as a glorious opportunity to serve God and to do His will? Are you enthused about life, or do you struggle through each day giving scarcely a thought to God's blessings? Are you constantly praising God for His gifts, and are you sharing His Good News with the world? And are you excited about the possibilities for service that God has placed before you, whether at home, at work, or at church? You should be.

You are the recipient of Christ's sacrificial love. Accept it enthusiastically and share it fervently. Jesus deserves your enthusiasm; the world deserves it; and you deserve the experience of sharing it.

More from God's Word

Never be lazy in your work, but serve the Lord enthusiastically.

Romans 12:11 NLT

Whatever work you do, do your best, because you are going to the grave, where there is no working . . . .

Ecclesiastes 9:10 NCV

I have seen that there is nothing better than for a person to enjoy his activities, because that is his reward. For who can enable him to see what will happen after he dies?

Ecclesiastes 3:22 HCSB

Do your work with enthusiasm. Work as if you were serving the Lord, not as if you were serving only men and women.

Ephesians 6:7 NCV

But those who wait on the LORD shall renew their strength; they shall mount up with wings like eagles, they shall run and not be weary, they shall walk and not faint.

Isaiah 40:31 NKJV

More Ideas for Your Journey

When we wholeheartedly commit ourselves to God, there is nothing mediocre or run-of-the-mill about us. To live for Christ is to be passionate about our Lord and about our lives.

Jim Gallery

Wherever you are, be all there. Live to the hilt every situation you believe to be the will of God.

Jim Elliot

Catch on fire with enthusiasm and people will come for miles to watch you burn.

John Wesley

A Father's Prayer

Dear Lord, You have called me not to a life of mediocrity, but to a life of passion. Today, I will be an enthusiastic follower of Your Son, and I will share His Good News—and His love—with all who cross my path. Amen

The Need to Lead

Shepherd God's flock among you, not overseeing out of compulsion but freely, according to God's will; not for the money but eagerly.

1 Peter 5:2 HCSB

As the leader of your family, you have a profound responsibility to your loved ones and to your God. If you desire to be an obedient servant to your Heavenly Father, you must lead your family according to His Holy Word. To do otherwise is to rob your loved ones of the peace and abundance that is rightfully theirs through the person of Jesus Christ.

Our world needs Christian leaders, and so does your family. So make this pledge and keep it: vow to become the godly leader that God intends you to be. Your family needs you, and you need the experience of leading them in the service of our Lord.

More from God's Word

According to the grace given to us, we have different gifts: If prophecy, use it according to the standard of faith; if service, in service; if teaching, in teaching; if exhorting, in exhortation; giving, with generosity; leading, with diligence; showing mercy, with cheerfulness.

Romans 12:6-8 HCSB

And we exhort you, brothers: warn those who are lazy, comfort the discouraged, help the weak, be patient with everyone.

1 Thessalonians 5:14 HCSB

His master said to him, "Well done, good and faithful slave! You were faithful over a few things; I will put you in charge of many things. Enter your master's joy!"

Matthew 25:21 HCSB

Good leadership is a channel of water controlled by God; he directs it to whatever ends he chooses.

Proverbs 21:1 MSG

More Ideas for Your Journey

The test of a leader is taking the vision from me to we.

John Maxwell

What do we Christians chiefly value in our leaders? The answer seems to be not their holiness, but their gifts and skills and resources. The thought that only holy people are likely to be spiritually useful does not loom large in our minds.

J. I. Packer

The goal of leadership is to empower the whole people of God to discern and to discharge the Lord's will.

Stanley Grenz

A Father's Prayer

Dear Lord, when I find myself in a position of leadership, let me seek Your will and obey Your commandments. Make me a person of integrity and wisdom, Lord, and make me a worthy example to my family. Let me be a Christ-centered leader, and let me turn to You, Father, for guidance, for courage, for wisdom, and for love. Amen

Using Your Gifts

I remind you to keep ablaze the gift of God that is in you.

2 Timothy 1:6 HCSB

Your talents are a gift from God. And, the same applies to your children. Their talents, too, are blessings from the Creator, blessings which must be nurtured or forfeited.

Are you and your loved ones willing to use your gifts in the way that God intends? Are you willing to summon the discipline that is required to develop your talents and to hone your skills? That's precisely what God wants you to do, and that's precisely what you should desire for yourselves.

So be faithful stewards of your talents and treasures. And then prepare yourselves for even greater blessings that are sure to come.

More Ideas for Your Journey

God often reveals His direction for our lives through the way He made us…with a certain personality and unique skills.

Bill Hybels

You are the only person on earth who can use your ability.

Zig Ziglar

Employ whatever God has entrusted you with, in doing good, all possible good, in every possible kind and degree.

John Wesley

A Father's Prayer

Dear Lord, let me use my gifts, and let me help my children discover theirs. Your gifts are priceless and eternal—may we, as Your faithful children, use our own gifts to the glory of Your kingdom, today and forever. Amen

Too Many Distractions?

Look straight ahead, and fix your eyes on what lies before you. Mark out a straight path for your feet; then stick to the path and stay safe. Don't get sidetracked; keep your feet from following evil.

Proverbs 4:25-27 NLT

All of us must live through those days when the traffic jams, the computer crashes, and the dog makes a main course out of our homework. But, when we find ourselves distracted by the minor frustrations of life, we must catch ourselves, take a deep breath, and lift our thoughts upward.

Although we may, at times, struggle mightily to rise above the distractions of the everyday living, we need never struggle alone. God is here—eternal and faithful, with infinite patience and love—and, if we reach out to Him, He will restore our sense of perspective and give peace to our souls.

More from God's Word

Let us lay aside every weight and the sin that so easily ensnares us, and run with endurance the race that lies before us, keeping our eyes on Jesus, the source and perfecter of our faith.

Hebrews 12:1-2 HCSB

Give your entire attention to what God is doing right now, and don't get worked up about what may or may not happen tomorrow. God will help you deal with whatever hard things come up when the time comes.

Matthew 6:34 MSG

Don't look for shortcuts to God. The market is flooded with surefire, easygoing formulas for a successful life that can be practiced in your spare time. Don't fall for that stuff, even though crowds of people do. The way to life—to God!—is vigorous and requires total attention.

Matthew 7:13-14 MSG

So let's keep focused on that goal [reaching out to Christ], those of us who want everything God has for us. If any of you have something else in mind, something less than total commitment, God will clear your blurred vision, you'll see it yet!

Philippians 3:15, 16 MSG

More Ideas for Your Journey

As long as Jesus is one of many options, he is no option.

Max Lucado

Only the man who follows the command of Jesus single-mindedly and unresistingly let his yoke rest upon him, finds his burden easy, and under its gentle pressure receives the power to persevere in the right way.

Dietrich Bonhoeffer

Paul did one thing. Most of us dabble in forty things. Are you a doer or a dabbler?

Vance Havner

A Father's Prayer

Dear Lord, help me to face this day with a spirit of optimism and thanksgiving. And let me focus my thoughts on You and Your incomparable gifts. Amen

You and Your Conscience

If the way you live isn't consistent with what you believe, then it's wrong.

Romans 14:23 MSG

B illy Graham correctly observed, "Most of us follow our conscience as we follow a wheelbarrow. We push it in front of us in the direction we want to go." To do so, of course, is a profound mistake. Yet all of us, on occasion, have failed to listen to the voice that God planted in our hearts, and all of us have suffered the consequences.

God gave you a conscience for a very good reason: to make your path conform to His will. Wise believers make it a practice to listen carefully to that quiet internal voice. Count yourself among that number. When your conscience speaks, listen and learn. In all likelihood, God is trying to get His message through. And in all likelihood, it is a message that you desperately need to hear.

More from God's Word

Now the goal of our instruction is love from a pure heart, a good conscience, and a sincere faith.

1 Timothy 1:5 HCSB

I always do my best to have a clear conscience toward God and men.

Acts 24:16 HCSB

Let us draw near with a true heart in full assurance of faith, our hearts sprinkled clean from an evil conscience and our bodies washed in pure water.

Hebrews 10:22 HCSB

I will cling to my righteousness and never let it go. My conscience will not accuse [me] as long as I live!

Job 27:6 HCSB

Behold, the kingdom of God is within you.

Luke 17:21 KJV

More Ideas for Your Journey

To go against one's conscience is neither safe nor right. Here I stand. I cannot do otherwise.

Martin Luther

The convicting work of the Holy Spirit awakens, disturbs, and judges.

Franklin Graham

The beginning of backsliding means your conscience does not answer to the truth.

Oswald Sanders

A Father's Prayer

Dear Lord, You speak to me through the gift of Your Holy Word. And, Father, You speak to me through that still small voice that tells me right from wrong. Let me follow Your way, Lord, and, in these quiet moments, show me Your plan for this day, that I might serve You. Amen

Embracing God's Love

Unfailing love surrounds those who trust the LORD.

Psalm 32:10 NLT

As Christian dads who have been saved by God's grace, we have a profound responsibility to educate our children in the ways of the Lord. God is a loving Father. We are God's children, and we are called upon to be faithful to Him.

When we embrace God's love, we are forever changed. When we embrace God's love, we feel differently about our neighbors, our world, and ourselves. When we embrace God's love, we tell and retell the wondrous story of His Son.

We return our Father's love by sharing it with others. We honor our Heavenly Father by obeying His commandments and sharing His Good News. When we do, we are blessed…and the Father smiles.

More from God's Word

We love Him because He first loved us.

1 John 4:19 NKJV

Draw near to God, and He will draw near to you.

James 4:8 HCSB

For He is gracious and compassionate, slow to anger, rich in faithful love.

Joel 2:13 HCSB

For God loved the world in this way: He gave His only Son, so that everyone who believes in Him will not perish but have eternal life.

John 3:16 HCSB

For the Lord is good, and His love is eternal; His faithfulness endures through all generations.

Psalm 100:5 HCSB

More Ideas for Your Journey

If you have an obedience problem, you have a love problem. Focus your attention on God's love.

Henry Blackaby

Even when we cannot see the why and wherefore of God's dealings, we know that there is love in and behind them, so we can rejoice always.

J. I. Packer

The life of faith is a daily exploration of the constant and countless ways in which God's grace and love are experienced.

Eugene Peterson

A Father's Prayer

Thank You, Dear God, for Your love. You are my loving Father. I thank You for Your love and for Your Son. I will praise You; I will worship You; and I will love You today, tomorrow, and forever. Amen

A Happy Christian

Happy are the people whose strength is in You, whose hearts are set on pilgrimage.

Psalm 84:5 HCSB

Happiness depends less upon our circumstances than upon our thoughts. When we turn our thoughts to God, to His gifts, and to His glorious creation, we experience the joy that God intends for His children. But, when we focus on the negative aspects of life, we suffer needlessly.

Do you sincerely want to be a happy Christian? Then set your mind and your heart upon God's love and His grace. The fullness of life in Christ is available to all who seek it and claim it. Count yourself among that number. Seek first the salvation that is available through a personal relationship with Jesus Christ, and then claim the joy, the peace, and the spiritual abundance that the Shepherd offers His sheep.

More Ideas for Your Journey

There is no correlation between wealth and happiness.

Larry Burkett

Our thoughts, not our circumstances, determine our happiness.

John Maxwell

Whoever possesses God is happy.

St. Augustine

A Father's Prayer

Dear Lord, You are my strength and my joy. I will rejoice in the day that You have made, and I will give thanks for the countless blessings that You have given me. Let me be a joyful Christian, Father, as I share Your Good News with friends, with family, and with the world. Amen

What a Friend

Therefore if any man be in Christ, he is a new creature: old things are passed away; behold, all things are become new.

2 Corinthians 5:17 KJV

Our circumstances change but Jesus does not. Even when the world seems to be trembling between our feet, Jesus remains the spiritual bedrock that cannot be moved.

The old familiar hymn begins, "What a friend we have in Jesus...." No truer words were ever penned. Jesus is the sovereign Friend and ultimate Savior of mankind. Christ showed enduring love for His believers by willingly sacrificing His own life so that we might have eternal life. Let us love Him, praise Him, and share His message of salvation with our neighbors and with the world.

More from God's Word

The next day John saw Jesus coming toward him and said, "Here is the Lamb of God, who takes away the sin of the world!

John 1:29 HCSB

But we do see Jesus—made lower than the angels for a short time so that by God's grace He might taste death for everyone—crowned with glory and honor because of the suffering of death.

Hebrews 2:9 HCSB

For unto us a Child is born, Unto us a Son is given; And the government will be upon His shoulder. And His name will be called Wonderful, Counselor, Mighty God, Everlasting Father, Prince of Peace.

Isaiah 9:6 NKJV

In the beginning was the Word, and the Word was with God, and the Word was God.... And the Word was made flesh, and dwelt among us, (and we beheld his glory, the glory as of the only begotten of the Father,) full of grace and truth.

John 1:1, 14 KJV

More Ideas for Your Journey

Jesus came into the world so we could know, once and for all, that God is concerned about the way we live, the way we believe, and the way we die.

Billy Graham

Jesus: the proof of God's love.

Philip Yancey

Jesus was the perfect reflection of God's nature in every situation He encountered during His time here on earth.

Bill Hybels

A Father's Prayer

Heavenly Father, I praise You for Your Son. Jesus is my Savior and my strength. Let me share His Good News with all who cross my path, and let me share His love with all who need His healing touch. Amen

Obedience Now

You must follow the Lord your God and fear Him. You must keep His commands and listen to His voice; you must worship Him and remain faithful to Him.

Deuteronomy 13:4 HCSB

God's laws are eternal and unchanging: obedience leads to abundance and joy; disobedience leads to disaster. God has given us a guidebook for righteous living called the Holy Bible. If we trust God's Word and live by it, we are blessed. But, if we choose to ignore God's commandments, the results are as predictable as they are tragic.

Life is a series of decisions and choices. Each day, we make countless decisions that can bring us closer to God...or not. When we live according to God's commandments, we earn for ourselves the abundance and peace that He intends for our lives.

Do you seek God's peace and His blessings? Then obey Him. When you're faced with a difficult choice or a powerful temptation, seek God's counsel and trust the counsel He gives. Invite God into your heart and live according to His commandments. When you do, you will be blessed today, and tomorrow, and forever.

More from God's Word

Therefore, get your minds ready for action, being self-disciplined, and set your hope completely on the grace to be brought to you at the revelation of Jesus Christ. As obedient children, do not be conformed to the desires of your former ignorance but, as the One who called you is holy, you also are to be holy in all your conduct.

1 Peter 1:13-15 HCSB

But whoever keeps His word, truly the love of God is perfected in him. By this we know that we are in Him. He who says he abides in Him ought himself also to walk just as He walked.

1 John 2:5-6 NKJV

Because the eyes of the Lord are on the righteous and His ears are open to their request. But the face of the Lord is against those who do evil.

1 Peter 3:12 HCSB

More Ideas for Your Journey

Believe and do what God says. The life-changing consequences will be limitless, and the results will be confidence and peace of mind.

Franklin Graham

All true knowledge of God is born out of obedience.

John Calvin

Obedience is the outward expression of your love of God.

Henry Blackaby

A Father's Prayer

Lord, my family is both a priceless gift and a profound responsibility. Let my actions be worthy of that responsibility. Lead me along Your path, Lord, and guide me far from the frustrations and distractions of this troubled world. Let Your Holy Word guide my actions, and let Your love reside in my heart, this day and every day. Amen

Caring for Your Family

Whoever does not care for his own relatives, especially his own family members, has turned against the faith and is worse than someone who does not believe in God.

1 Timothy 5:8 NCV

The words of 1 Timothy 5:8 are unambiguous: if God has blessed us with families, then He expects us to care for them. Sometimes, this profound responsibility seems daunting. And sometimes, even for the most dedicated Christian men, family life holds moments of frustration and disappointment. But, for those who are lucky enough to live in the presence of a close-knit, caring clan, the rewards far outweigh the demands.

No family is perfect, and neither is yours. Despite the inevitable challenges of providing for your family, and despite the occasional hurt feelings of family life, your clan is God's gift to you. Give thanks to the Giver for the gift of family...and act accordingly.

More Ideas for Your Journey

It is a reverent thing to see an ancient castle or building not in decay, or to see a fair timber tree sound and perfect. How much more beautiful it is to behold an ancient and noble family that has stood against the waves and weathers of time.

Francis Bacon

Never give your family the leftovers and crumbs of your time.

Charles Swindoll

The only true source of meaning in life is found in love for God and his son Jesus Christ, and love for mankind, beginning with our own families.

James Dobson

A Father's Prayer

Lord, You have given me a family to love and to care for. Thank You, Father. I will love all the members of my family despite their imperfections. Let them love me, Dear Lord, despite mine. Amen

Sharing Your Faith

But sanctify the Lord God in your hearts, and always be ready to give a defense to everyone who asks you a reason for the hope that is in you.

1 Peter 3:15 HCSB

Our personal testimonies are extremely important, but sometimes, because of shyness or insecurities, we're afraid to share our experiences. And that's unfortunate.

In his second letter to Timothy, Paul shares a message to believers of every generation when he writes, "God has not given us a spirit of timidity" (1:7). Paul's meaning is clear: When sharing our beliefs, we, as Christians, must be courageous, forthright, and unashamed.

We live in a world that desperately needs the healing message of Christ Jesus. Every believer, each in his or her own way, bears responsibility for sharing the Good News of our Savior.

Billy Graham observed, "Our faith grows by expression. If we want to keep our faith, we must share it." If you are a follower of Christ, the time to express your belief in Him is now. You know how He has touched your heart; help Him do the same for others.

More Ideas for Your Journey

To take up the cross means that you take your stand for the Lord Jesus no matter what it costs.

Billy Graham

To stand in an uncaring world and say, "See, here is the Christ" is a daring act of courage.

Calvin Miller

The sermon of your life in tough times ministers to people more powerfully than the most eloquent speaker.

Bill Bright

A Father's Prayer

Lord, the life that I live and the words that I speak will tell my family and the world how I feel about You. Today and every day, let my testimony be worthy of You. Let my words be sure and true, and let my actions point others to You. Amen

The Wisdom to Be Humble

For everyone who exalts himself will be humbled, and the one who humbles himself will be exalted.

Luke 14:11 HCSB

Hopefully, you are a proud papa. God intends that you take appropriate parental pride in every member of your family. But God has a stern warning for those who would take undo pride in their own accomplishments. Excessive pride is a sin.

As Christians, we have a profound reason to be humble: We have been refashioned and saved by Jesus Christ, and that salvation came not because of our own good works but because of God's grace. Thus, we are not "self-made"; we are "God-made" and "Christ-saved." How, then, can we be boastful? The answer, of course, is simple: if we are to be honest with ourselves and with our God, we cannot be boastful. In the quiet moments, when we search the depths of our own hearts, we know that whatever "it" is, God did that. And He deserves the credit.

More from God's Word

Clothe yourselves with humility toward one another, because God resists the proud, but gives grace to the humble.

1 Peter 5:5 HCSB

But He said to me, "My grace is sufficient for you, for power is perfected in weakness." Therefore, I will most gladly boast all the more about my weaknesses, so that Christ's power may reside in me.

2 Corinthians 12:9 HCSB

You will save the humble people; but Your eyes are on the haughty, that You may bring them down.

2 Samuel 22:28 NKJV

If My people who are called by My name will humble themselves, and pray and seek My face, and turn from their wicked ways, then I will hear from heaven, and will forgive their sin and heal their land.

2 Chronicles 7:14 NKJV

Do nothing out of rivalry or conceit, but in humility consider others as more important than yourselves.

Philippians 2:3 HCSB

More Ideas for Your Journey

God exalts humility. When God works in our lives, helping us to become humble, he gives us a permanent joy. Humility gives us a joy that cannot be taken away.

Max Lucado

It was pride that changed angels into devils; it is humility that makes men as angels.

St. Augustine

Humility is not thinking less of yourself; it is thinking of yourself less.

Rick Warren

A Father's Prayer

Heavenly Father, Jesus clothed Himself with humility when He chose to leave heaven and come to earth to live and die for us, His children. Christ is my Master and my example. Clothe me with humility, Lord, so that I might be more like Your Son, and keep me mindful that You are the giver and sustainer of life, and to You, Dear Lord, goes the glory and the praise. Amen

Answering the Call

I, therefore, the prisoner in the Lord, urge you to walk worthy of the calling you have received.

Ephesians 4:1 HCSB

It is vitally important that you heed God's call. In John 15:16, Jesus says, "You did not choose me, but I chose you and appointed you to go and bear fruit—fruit that will last" (NIV). In other words, you have been called by Christ, and now, it is up to you to decide precisely how you will answer.

Have you already found your special calling? If so, you're a very lucky guy. If not, keep searching and keep praying until you discover it. And remember this: God has important work for you to do—work that no one else on earth can accomplish but you.

More from God's Word

But as God has distributed to each one, as the Lord has called each one, so let him walk.

1 Corinthians 7:17 NKJV

I pray that the eyes of your heart may be enlightened so you may know what is the hope of His calling, what are the glorious riches of His inheritance among the saints, and what is the immeasurable greatness of His power to us who believe, according to the working of His vast strength.

Ephesians 1:18-19 HCSB

So the last shall be first, and the first last: for many be called, but few chosen.

Matthew 20:16 KJV

One thing I do, forgetting those things which are behind and reaching forward to those things which are ahead, I press toward the goal for the prize of the upward call of God in Christ Jesus.

Philippians 3:13-14 NKJV

I remind you to keep ablaze the gift of God that is in you.

2 Timothy 1:6 HCSB

More Ideas for Your Journey

The world does not consider labor a blessing, therefore it flees and hates it, but the pious who fear the Lord labor with a ready and cheerful heart, for they know God's command, and they acknowledge His calling.

Martin Luther

If God has called you, do not spend time looking over your shoulder to see who is following you.

Corrie ten Boom

When you become consumed by God's call on your life, everything will take on new meaning and significance. You will begin to see every facet of your life, including your pain, as a means through which God can work to bring others to Himself.

Charles Stanley

A Father's Prayer

Heavenly Father, You have called me, and I acknowledge that calling. In these quiet moments before this busy day unfolds, I come to You. I will study Your Word and seek Your guidance. Give me the wisdom to know Your will for my life and the courage to follow wherever You may lead me, today and forever. Amen

He Keeps His Promises

Let us hold on to the confession of our hope without wavering, for He who promised is faithful.

Hebrews 10:23 HCSB

God has made quite a few promises to you, and He intends to keep every single one of them. You will find these promises in a book like no other: the Holy Bible. The Bible is your guide for life here on earth and for life eternal—as a believer, you are called upon to trust its promises, to follow its commandments, and to share its Good News.

God has made promises to all of humanity and to you. God's promises never fail and they never grow old. You must trust those promises and share them with your family, with your friends, and with the world . . . starting now . . . and ending never.

More Ideas for Your Journey

There are four words I wish we would never forget, and they are, "God keeps his word."

Charles Swindoll

The stars may fall, but God's promises will stand and be fulfilled.

J. I. Packer

God's promises are overflowings from his great heart.

C. H. Spurgeon

A Father's Prayer

Lord, Your Holy Word contains promises, and I will trust them. I will use the Bible as my guide, and I will trust You, Lord, to speak to me through Your Holy Spirit and through Your Holy Word, this day and forever. Amen

Accepting His Peace

And the peace of God, which surpasses every thought, will guard your hearts and your minds in Christ Jesus. Finally brothers, whatever is true, whatever is honorable, whatever is just, whatever is pure, whatever is lovely, whatever is commendable—if there is any moral excellence and if there is any praise—dwell on these things.

Philippians 4:7-8 HCSB

As a busy father, your plate is probably full: kids to care for, bills to pay, a family to lead. Sometimes it seems that you can scarcely find a moment's peace. But the beautiful words of John 14:27 are a reminder that God's peace is always available to you.

Jesus said, "Peace I leave with you, my peace I give unto you . . . ." Christ offers us peace, not as the world gives, but as He alone gives. We, as believers, can accept His peace or ignore it.

When we accept the peace of Jesus Christ into our hearts, our lives are transformed. And then, because we possess the gift of peace, we can share that gift with fellow Christians, family members, friends, and associates.

If, on the other hand, we choose to ignore the gift of peace—for whatever reason—we simply cannot share what we do not possess.

Today, as a gift to yourself, to your family, and to your friends, claim the inner peace that is your spiritual birthright: the peace of Jesus Christ. It is offered freely; it has been paid for in full; it is yours for the asking. So ask. And then share.

More from God's Word

Abundant peace belongs to those who love Your instruction; nothing makes them stumble.

Psalm 119:165 HCSB

Blessed are the peacemakers, for they shall be called sons of God.

Matthew 5:9 NKJV

And suddenly there was with the angel a multitude of the heavenly host praising God and saying: "Glory to God in the highest, and on earth peace, goodwill toward men!"

Luke 2:13-14 NKJV

More Ideas for Your Journey

A great many people are trying to make peace, but that has already been done. God has not left it for us to do; all we have to do is to enter into it.

D. L. Moody

The Bible instructs—and experience teaches—that praising God results in our burdens being lifted and our joys being multiplied.

Jim Gallery

For Jesus peace seems to have meant not the absence of struggle but the presence of love.

Frederick Buechner

A Father's Prayer

Dear Lord, the peace that the world offers is fleeting, but You offer a peace that is perfect and eternal. Let me take my concerns and burdens to You, Father, and let me feel the spiritual abundance that You offer through the person of Your Son, the Prince of Peace. Amen

He's Here

The Lord is near all who call out to Him, all who call out to Him with integrity. He fulfills the desires of those who fear Him; He hears their cry for help and saves them.

Psalm 145:18-19 HCSB

Where is God? God is eternally with us. He is omnipresent. He is, quite literally, everywhere you have ever been and everywhere you will ever go. He is with you night and day; He knows your every thought; He hears your every heartbeat.

Sometimes, in the crush of your daily duties, God may seem far away. Or sometimes, when the disappointments and sorrows of life leave you brokenhearted, God may seem distant, but He is not. When you earnestly seek God, you will find Him because He is here, waiting patiently for you to reach out to Him . . . right here . . . right now.

More from God's Word

Come near to God, and God will come near to you. You sinners, clean sin out of your lives. You who are trying to follow God and the world at the same time, make your thinking pure.

James 4:8 NCV

No, I will not abandon you as orphans—I will come to you.

John 14:18 NLT

Again, this is God's command: to believe in his personally named Son, Jesus Christ. He told us to love each other, in line with the original command. As we keep his commands, we live deeply and surely in him, and he lives in us. And this is how we experience his deep and abiding presence in us: by the Spirit he gave us.

1 John 3:23-24 MSG

Fear not, for I am with you; be not dismayed, for I am your God. I will strengthen you.

Isaiah 41:10 NKJV

I am not alone, because the Father is with Me.

John 16:32 HCSB

More Ideas for Your Journey

There is a basic urge: the longing for unity. You desire a reunion with God—with God your Father.

E. Stanley Jones

The next time you hear a baby laugh or see an ocean wave, take note. Pause and listen as his Majesty whispers ever so gently, "I'm here."

Max Lucado

Get yourself into the presence of the loving Father. Just place yourself before Him, and look up into, His face; think of His love, His wonderful, tender, pitying love.

Andrew Murray

A Father's Prayer

Dear Lord, You are with me always. Help me feel Your presence in every situation and every circumstance. Today, Dear God, let me feel You and acknowledge Your presence, Your love, and Your Son. Amen

His Golden Rule

Do to others as you would have them do to you.

Luke 6:31 NIV

Some rules are easier to understand than they are to live by. Jesus told us that we should treat other people in the same way that we want to be treated: that's the Golden Rule. But sometimes, especially when we're feeling pressure from friends, or when we're tired or upset, obeying the Golden Rule can seem like an impossible task—but it's not.

God wants us to treat other people with respect, kindness, and courtesy. He wants us to rise above our own imperfections, and He wants us to treat others with unselfishness and love. To make it short and sweet, God wants us to obey the Golden Rule, and He knows we can do it.

So if you're wondering how to treat someone else, ask the person you see every time you look into the mirror. The answer you receive will tell you exactly what to do.

More Ideas for Your Journey

The mark of a Christian is that he will walk the second mile and turn the other cheek. A wise man or woman gives the extra effort, all for the glory of the Lord Jesus Christ.

John Maxwell

When you extend hospitality to others, you're not trying to impress people, you're trying to reflect God to them.

Max Lucado

Faith never asks whether good works are to be done, but has done them before there is time to ask the question, and it is always doing them.

Martin Luther

A Father's Prayer

Dear Lord, the Golden Rule is not only a perfect standard to use with my friends and neighbors, it is also a guide for raising my children. Enable me to respect my children as I want them to respect me. Help me to walk in their shoes and to see life from their perspective. Help me, Father, to be a nurturing, loving parent every day that I live, and may the glory be yours. Amen

Time for Fun

So I recommend having fun, because there is nothing better for people to do in this world than to eat, drink, and enjoy life. That way they will experience some happiness along with all the hard work God gives them.

Ecclesiastes 8:15 NLT

Are you a man who takes time each day to really enjoy life? Hopefully so. After all, you are the recipient of a precious gift—the gift of life. And because God has seen fit to give you this gift, it is incumbent upon you to use it and to enjoy it. But sometimes, amid the inevitable pressures of everyday living, really enjoying life may seem almost impossible. It is not.

For most of us, fun is as much a function of attitude as it is a function of environment. So whether you're standing victorious atop one of life's mountains or trudging through one of life's valleys, enjoy yourself. You deserve to have fun today, and God wants you to have fun today . . . so what on earth are you waiting for?

More Ideas for Your Journey

If we don't hunger and thirst after righteousness, we'll become anemic and feel miserable in our Christian experience.

Franklin Graham

True happiness and contentment cannot come from the things of this world. The blessedness of true joy is a free gift that comes only from our Lord and Savior, Jesus Christ.

Dennis Swanberg

The happiest people in the world are not those who have no problems, but the people who have learned to live with those things that are less than perfect.

James Dobson

A Father's Prayer

Dear Lord, You are my strength and my joy. I will rejoice in the day that You have made, and I will give thanks for the countless blessings that You have given me. Let me be a joyful Christian, Father, as I share the Good News of Your Son, and let me praise You for all the marvelous things You have done. Amen

Time for God

Don't burn out; keep yourselves fueled and aflame. Be alert servants of the Master, cheerfully expectant. Don't quit in hard times; pray all the harder.

Romans 12:11-12 MSG

Has the busy pace of life robbed you of the peace that might otherwise be yours through Jesus Christ? If so, you are simply too busy for your own good. Through His Son Jesus, God offers you a peace that passes human understanding, but He won't force His peace upon you; in order to experience it, you must slow down long enough to sense His presence and His love.

Today, as a gift to yourself, to your family, and to the world, slow down and claim the inner peace that is your spiritual birthright: the peace of Jesus Christ. It is offered freely; it has been paid for in full; it is yours for the asking. So ask. And then share.

More from God's Word

Come to Me, all you who are weary and burdened, and I will give you rest. Take My yoke upon you and learn from Me, because I am gentle and humble in heart, and you will find rest for your souls. For My yoke is easy and My burden is light.

Matthew 11:28-30 HCSB

Careful planning puts you ahead in the long run; hurry and scurry puts you further behind.

Proverbs 21:5 MSG

You can't go wrong when you love others. When you add up everything in the law code, the sum total is love. But make sure that you don't get so absorbed and exhausted in taking care of all your day-by-day obligations that you lose track of the time and doze off, oblivious to God.

Romans 13:10-11 MSG

Jesus said, "You're tied down to the mundane; I'm in touch with what is beyond your horizons. You live in terms of what you see and touch. I'm living on other terms. I told you that you were missing God in all this. You're at a dead end. If you won't believe I am who I say I am, you're at the dead end of sins. You're missing God in your lives."

John 8:23-24 MSG

More Ideas for Your Journey

Busyness is the great enemy of relationships.

Rick Warren

Being busy, in and of itself, is not a sin. But being busy in an endless pursuit of things that leave us empty and hollow and broken inside—that cannot be pleasing to God.

Max Lucado

This is a day when we are so busy doing everything that we have no time to be anything. Even religiously we are so occupied with activities that we have no time to know God.

Vance Havner

A Father's Prayer

Dear Lord, sometimes, I am distracted by the busyness of the day or the demands of the moment. When I am worried or anxious, Father, turn my thoughts back to You. Help me to trust Your will, to follow Your commands, and to accept Your peace, today and forever. Amen

Your Own Worst Critic?

Those who wait for perfect weather will never plant seeds; those who look at every cloud will never harvest crops. Plant early in the morning, and work until evening, because you don't know if this or that will succeed. They might both do well.

Ecclesiastes 11:4, 6 NCV

When God made you, He equipped you with an array of talents and abilities that are uniquely yours. It's up to you to discover those talents and to use them, but sometimes your own perfectionism may get in the way.

If you're your own worst critic, give it up. After all, God doesn't expect you to be perfect, and if that's okay with Him, then it should be okay with you, too.

When you accepted Christ as your Savior, God accepted you for all eternity. Now, it's your turn to accept yourself. When you do, you'll feel a tremendous weight being lifted from your shoulders. And that's as it should be. After all, only one earthly being ever lived life to perfection, and He was the Son of God. The rest of us have fallen short of God's standard and need to be accepting of our own limitations as well as the limitations of others.

More from God's Word

For You have made him a little lower than the angels, and You have crowned him with glory and honor.

Psalm 8:5 NKJV

How happy are those whose way is blameless, who live according to the law of the Lord! Happy are those who keep His decrees and seek Him with all their heart.

Psalm 119:1-2 HCSB

Happy is the one whose help is the God of Jacob, whose hope is in the Lord his God.

Psalm 146:5 HCSB

Finally, brethren, whatever things are true, whatever things are noble, whatever things are just, whatever things are pure, whatever things are lovely, whatever things are of good report, if there is any virtue and if there is anything praiseworthy— meditate on these things.

Philippians 4:8 NKJV

More Ideas for Your Journey

The happiest people in the world are not those who have no problems, but the people who have learned to live with those things that are less than perfect.

James Dobson

I want you to remember what a difference there is between perfection and perfectionism. The former is a Bible truth; the latter may or may not be a human perversion of the truth. I fear that many, in their horror of perfectionism, reject perfection too.

Andrew Murray

What makes a Christian a Christian is not perfection but forgiveness.

Max Lucado

A Father's Prayer

Lord, this world has so many expectations of me, but today I will not seek to meet the world's expectations; I will do my best to meet Your expectations. I will make You my ultimate priority, Lord, by serving You, by praising You, by loving You, and by obeying You. Amen

Devotion 69

The Ultimate Armor

If God is for us, who is against us?

Romans 8:31 HCSB

God has promised to protect us, and He intends to keep His promise. In a world filled with dangers and temptations, God is the ultimate armor. In a world filled with misleading messages, God's Word is the ultimate truth. In a world filled with more frustrations than we can count, God's Son offers the ultimate peace.

Will you accept God's peace and wear God's armor against the dangers of our world? Hopefully so—because when you do, you can live courageously, knowing that you possess the ultimate protection: God's unfailing love for you.

More from God's Word

The Lord is my rock, my fortress, and my deliverer, my God, my mountain where I seek refuge. My shield, the horn of my salvation, my stronghold, my refuge, and my Savior.

2 Samuel 22:2-3 HCSB

God—His way is perfect; the word of the Lord is pure. He is a shield to all who take refuge in Him.

Psalm 18:30 HCSB

The Lord is my rock, my fortress, and my deliverer.

Psalm 18:2 HCSB

The Lord bless you and protect you; the Lord make His face shine on you, and be gracious to you.

Numbers 6:24-25 HCSB

I know whom I have believed and am persuaded that He is able to guard what has been entrusted to me until that day.

2 Timothy 1:12 HCSB

More Ideas for Your Journey

The Rock of Ages is the great sheltering encirclement.

Oswald Chambers

Under heaven's lock and key, we are protected by the most efficient security system available: the power of God.

Charles Swindoll

A mighty fortress is our God, a bulwark never failing / Our helper He, amid the flood of mortal ills prevailing / For still our ancient foe doth seek to work us woe / His craft and power are great, armed with cruel hate, / Our earth is not his equal.

Martin Luther

A Father's Prayer

Lord, sometimes life is difficult. Sometimes, I am worried, weary, or heartbroken. And sometimes, I encounter powerful temptations to disobey Your commandments. But, when I lift my eyes to You, Father, You strengthen me. When I am weak, You lift me up. Today, I will turn to You for strength, for hope, for direction, and for deliverance. Amen

Believe in Miracles

Looking at them, Jesus said, "With men it is impossible, but not with God, because all things are possible with God."

Mark 10:27 HCSB

Do you believe that God is at work in the world? And do you also believe that nothing is impossible for Him? If so, then you also believe that God is perfectly capable of doing things that you, as a mere human being with limited vision and limited understanding, would deem to be utterly impossible. And that's precisely what God does.

Since the moment that He created our universe out of nothingness, God has made a habit of doing miraculous things. And He still works miracles today. Expect Him to work miracles in your own life, and then be watchful. With God, absolutely nothing is impossible, including an amazing assortment of miracles that He stands ready, willing, and able to perform for you and yours.

More from God's Word

I assure you: The one who believes in Me will also do the works that I do. And he will do even greater works than these, because I am going to the Father.

John 14:12 HCSB

But as it is written: "Eye has not seen, nor ear heard, nor have entered into the heart of man the things which God has prepared for those who love Him."

1 Corinthians 2:9 NKJV

For nothing will be impossible with God.

Luke 1:37 HCSB

You are the God who works wonders; You revealed Your strength among the peoples.

Psalm 77:14 HCSB

Is anything impossible for the Lord?

Genesis 18:14 HCSB

More Ideas for Your Journey

Miracles are not contrary to nature but only contrary to what we know about nature.

St. Augustine

Only God can move mountains, but faith and prayer can move God.

E. M. Bounds

Too many Christians live below the miracle level.

Vance Havner

A Father's Prayer

Lord, for You, nothing is impossible. Let me trust in Your power to do the miraculous, and let me trust in Your willingness to work miracles in my life—and in my heart. Amen

Listen Carefully

The one who is from God listens to God's words. This is why you don't listen, because you are not from God.

John 8:47 HCSB

Sometimes God speaks loudly and clearly. More often, He speaks in a quiet voice—and if you are wise, you will be listening carefully when He does. To do so, you must carve out quiet moments each day to study His Word and sense His direction.

Can you quiet yourself long enough to listen to your conscience? Are you attuned to the subtle guidance of your intuition? Are you willing to pray sincerely and then to wait quietly for God's response? Hopefully so. Usually God refrains from sending His messages on stone tablets or city billboards. More often, He communicates in subtler ways. If you sincerely desire to hear His voice, you must listen carefully, and you must do so in the silent corners of your quiet, willing heart.

More from God's Word

Listen in silence before me....

Isaiah 41:1 NLT

God has no use for the prayers of the people who won't listen to him.

Proverbs 28:9 MSG

Trust God from the bottom of your heart; don't try to figure out everything on your own. Listen for God's voice in everything you do, everywhere you go; he's the one who will keep you on track.

Proverbs 3:5-6 MSG

You must follow the Lord your God and fear Him. You must keep His commands and listen to His voice; you must worship Him and remain faithful to Him.

Deuteronomy 13:4 HCSB

But as God has distributed to each one, as the Lord has called each one, so let him walk.

1 Corinthians 7:17 NKJV

More Ideas for Your Journey

In the soul-searching of our lives, we are to stay quiet so we can hear Him say all that He wants to say to us in our hearts.

Charles Swindoll

Listening is loving.

Zig Ziglar

We cannot experience the fullness of Christ if we do all the expressing. We must allow God to express His love, will, and truth to us.

Gary Smalley

A Father's Prayer

Lord, give me the wisdom to be a good listener. Help me listen carefully to my family, to my friends, and—most importantly—to You. Amen

Devotion 72

Watching the Donut

I can do everything through him that gives me strength.

Philippians 4:13 NIV

O n the wall of a little donut shop, the sign said:

As you travel through life, brother,
Whatever be your goal,
Keep your eye upon the donut,
And not upon the hole.

Do you keep your eye upon the donut, or have you acquired the bad habit of looking only at the hole? Hopefully, you spend most of your waking hours looking at the donut (and thanking God for it).

Christianity and pessimism don't mix. So do yourself a favor: choose to be a hope-filled Christian. Think optimistically about your life and your future. Trust your hopes, not your fears. Take time to celebrate God's glorious creation. And then, when you've filled your heart with hope and gladness, share your optimism with your friends. They'll be better for it, and so will you. But not necessarily in that order.

More from God's Word

Make your own attitude that of Christ Jesus.

Philippians 2:5 HCSB

Finally brothers, whatever is true, whatever is honorable, whatever is just, whatever is pure, whatever is lovely, whatever is commendable—if there is any moral excellence and if there is any praise—dwell on these things.

Philippians 4:8 HCSB

Set your minds on what is above, not on what is on the earth.

Colossians 3:2 HCSB

A cheerful heart has a continual feast.

Proverbs 15:15 HCSB

So I say to you, keep asking, and it will be given to you. Keep searching, and you will find. Keep knocking, and the door will be opened to you.

Luke 11:9 HCSB

More Ideas for Your Journey

The people whom I have seen succeed best in life have always been cheerful and hopeful people who went about their business with a smile on their faces.

Charles Kingsley

The essence of optimism is that it takes no account of the present, but it is a source of inspiration, of vitality, and of hope. Where others have resigned, it enables a man to hold his head high, to claim the future for himself, and not abandon it to his enemy.

Dietrich Bonhoeffer

Keep your feet on the ground, but let your heart soar as high as it will. Refuse to be average or to surrender to the chill of your spiritual environment.

A. W. Tozer

A Father's Prayer

Lord, let me be an expectant Christian. Let me expect the best from You, and let me look for the best in others. If I become discouraged, Father, turn my thoughts and my prayers to You. Let me trust You, Lord, to direct my life. And, let me share my faith and optimism with others, today and every day that I live. Amen

Family Worship

I rejoiced with those who said to me, "Let us go to the house of the Lord."

Psalm 122:1 HCSB

When you lead your family in worship, you are to be praised. By worshipping your Creator—and by teaching your children to do likewise—you make a powerful statement about the place that God occupies in your life.

Ours is a society in which too many men have abandoned the moral leadership of their families, often with tragic consequences. Men who neglect to worship God, either thoughtlessly or intentionally, invite untold suffering into their own lives and into the lives of their loved ones.

Every day provides opportunities to put God where He belongs: at the center of our hearts. May we worship Him, and only Him, always. And, may we encourage the members of our family to do the same.

More from God's Word

So that at the name of Jesus every knee should bow—of those who are in heaven and on earth and under the earth—and every tongue should confess that Jesus Christ is Lord, to the glory of God the Father.

Philippians 2:10-11 HCSB

Worship the Lord your God and . . . serve Him only.

Matthew 4:10 HCSB

If anyone is thirsty, he should come to Me and drink!

John 7:37 HCSB

But an hour is coming, and is now here, when the true worshipers will worship the Father in spirit and truth. Yes, the Father wants such people to worship Him. God is Spirit, and those who worship Him must worship in spirit and truth.

John 4:23-24 HCSB

Worship the Lord with gladness. Come before him, singing with joy. Acknowledge that the Lord is God! He made us, and we are his. We are his people, the sheep of his pasture.

Psalm 100:2-3 NLT

More Ideas for Your Journey

Worship is our response to the overtures of love from the heart of the Father.

Richard Foster

Because his spiritual existence transcends form, matter, and location, we have the freedom to worship him and experience his indwelling presence wherever we are.

R. C. Sproul

When God is at the center of your life, you worship. When he's not, you worry.

Rick Warren

A Father's Prayer

Heavenly Father, let today and every day be a time of worship for me and my family. Let us worship You, not only with words, but also with deeds. In the quiet moments of the day, let us praise You and thank You for creating us, loving us, guiding us, and saving us. Amen

Devotion 74

Fitness Matters

Whatever you eat or drink or whatever you do, you must do all for the glory of God.

1 Corinthians 10:31 NLT

Are you shaping up or spreading out? Do you eat sensibly and exercise regularly, or do you spend most of your time on the couch with a bag of chips in one hand and a clicker in the other? Are you choosing to treat your body like a temple or a trash heap? How you answer these questions will help determine how long you live and how well you live.

Physical fitness is a choice, a choice that requires discipline—it's as simple as that. So, do yourself this favor: treat your body like a one-of-a-kind gift from God . . . because that's precisely what your body is.

More Ideas for Your Journey

If you desire to improve your physical well-being and your emotional outlook, increasing your faith can help you.

John Maxwell

Jesus Christ is the One by Whom, for Whom, through Whom everything was made. Therefore, He knows what's wrong in your life and how to fix it.

Anne Graham Lotz

A Christian should no more defile his body than a Jew would defile the temple.

Warren Wiersbe

A Father's Prayer

Dear Lord, my body is Your temple—I will treat it with care. Amen

Genuine Contentment

I have learned to be content in whatever circumstances I am.
Philippians 4:11 HCSB

The preoccupation with happiness and content-ment is an ever-present theme in the modern world. We are bombarded with messages that tell us where to find peace and pleasure in a world that worships materialism and wealth. But, lasting content-ment is not found in material possessions; genuine con-tentment is a spiritual gift from God to those who trust in Him and follow His commandments.

Where can you and your family members find con-tentment? If you don't find it in God, you will never find it anywhere else. But, if you put your faith and your trust in Him, you will be blessed with an inner peace that is beyond human understanding. When God dwells at the center of your lives, peace and contentment will belong to you just as surely as you belong to God.

More from God's Word

A tranquil heart is life to the body, but jealousy is rottenness to the bones.

Proverbs 14:30 HCSB

The LORD will give strength to His people; the LORD will bless His people with peace.

Psalm 29:11 NKJV

Let your conduct be without covetousness; be content with such things as you have. For He Himself has said, "I will never leave you nor forsake you."

Hebrews 13:5 NKJV

But godliness with contentment is a great gain.

1 Timothy 6:6 HCSB

How happy are those whose way is blameless, who live according to the law of the Lord! Happy are those who keep His decrees and seek Him with all their heart.

Psalm 119:1-2 HCSB

More Ideas for Your Journey

He is truly happy who has all that he wishes to have, and wishes to have nothing that he ought not to have.

St. Augustine

The life of strain is difficult. The life of inner peace—a life that comes from a positive attitude—is the easiest type of existence.

Norman Vincent Peale

Contentment is not escape from battle, but rather an abiding peace and confidence in the midst of battle.

Warren Wiersbe

A Father's Prayer

Dear Lord, let me strive to do Your will here on earth, and as I do, let me find contentment and balance. Let me live in the light of Your will and Your priorities for my life. And let me teach my children the peace and contentment that can be theirs through the gift of Your Son. Amen

Real Repentance

The one who conceals his sins will not prosper, but whoever confesses and renounces them will find mercy.

Proverbs 28:13 HCSB

Who among us has sinned? All of us. But, God calls upon us to turn away from sin by following His commandments. And the good news is this: When we do ask for God's forgiveness and turn our hearts to Him, He forgives us absolutely and completely.

Genuine repentance requires more than simply offering God apologies for our misdeeds. Real repentance may start with feelings of sorrow and remorse, but it ends only when we turn away from the sin that has heretofore distanced us from our Creator. In truth, we offer our most meaningful apologies to God, not with our words, but with our actions. As long as we are still engaged in sin, we may be "repenting," but we have not fully "repented."

Is there an aspect of your life that is distancing you from God? If so, ask for His forgiveness, and—just as importantly—stop sinning. Then, wrap yourself in the protection of God's Word. When you do, you will be secure.

More from God's Word

If we say, "We have no sin," we are deceiving ourselves, and the truth is not in us. If we confess our sins, He is faithful and righteous to forgive us our sins and to cleanse us from all unrighteousness.

1 John 1:8-9 HCSB

When you are in distress and all these things have happened to you, you will return to the Lord your God in later days and obey Him. He will not leave you, destroy you, or forget the covenant with your fathers that He swore to them by oath, because the Lord your God is a compassionate God.

Deuteronomy 4:30-31 HCSB

But the Pharisees and their scribes were complaining to His disciples, "Why do you eat and drink with tax collectors and sinners?" Jesus replied to them, "The healthy don't need a doctor, but the sick do. I have not come to call the righteous, but sinners to repentance."

Luke 5:30-32 HCSB

More Ideas for Your Journey

But suppose we do sin. Suppose we slip and fall. Suppose we yield to temptation for a moment. What happens? We have to confess that sin.

Billy Graham

Repentance begins with confession of our guilt and recognition that our sin is against God.

Charles Stanley

Ten thousand confessions, if they do not spring from really contrite hearts, shall only be additions to their guilt.

C. H. Spurgeon

A Father's Prayer

When I stray from Your commandments, Lord, I must not only confess my sins, I must also turn from them. When I fall short, help me to change. When I reject Your Word and Your will for my life, guide me back to Your side. Forgive my sins, dear Lord, and help me live according to Your plan for my life. Your plan is perfect, Father; I am not. Let me trust in You. Amen

Being Generous

So let each one give as he purposes in his heart, not grudgingly or of necessity; for God loves a cheerful giver.

2 Corinthians 9:7 NKJV

God's gifts are beyond description, His blessings beyond comprehension. God has been incredibly generous with us, and He rightfully expects us to be generous with others. That's why the thread of generosity is woven into the very fabric of God's teachings.

In the Old Testament, we are told that, "The good person is generous and lends lavishly...." (Psalm 112:5 MSG). And in the New Testament we are instructed, "Freely you have received, freely give" (Matthew 10:8 NKJV). These principles still apply. As we establish priorities for our days and our lives, we are advised to give freely of our time, our possessions, and our love—just as God has given freely to us.

Of course, we can never fully repay God for His gifts, but we can share them with others. And we should.

More from God's Word

In every way I've shown you that by laboring like this, it is necessary to help the weak and to keep in mind the words of the Lord Jesus, for He said, "It is more blessed to give than to receive."

Acts 20:35 HCSB

Dear friend, you are showing your faith by whatever you do for the brothers, and this you are doing for strangers.

3 John 1:5 HCSB

Bear one another's burdens, and so fulfill the law of Christ.

Galatians 6:2 NKJV

If a brother or sister is without clothes and lacks daily food, and one of you says to them, "Go in peace, keep warm, and eat well," but you don't give them what the body needs, what good is it?

James 2:15–16 HCSB

The one who has two shirts must share with someone who has none, and the one who has food must do the same.

Luke 3:11 HCSB

More Ideas for Your Journey

Nothing is really ours until we share it.

C. S. Lewis

We are never more like God than when we give.

Charles Swindoll

If you want to be truly happy, you won't find it on an endless quest for more stuff. You'll find it in receiving God's generosity and then passing that generosity along.

Bill Hybels

A Father's Prayer

Dear Lord, You have been so generous with me; let me be generous with others. Help me to be generous with my time and my possessions as I care for those in need. Help me to teach my children to be cheerful givers, Father, and make us all humble givers, so that the glory and the praise might be Yours. Amen

Beyond Guilt

There is therefore now no condemnation to those who are in Christ Jesus, who do not walk according to the flesh, but according to the Spirit.

Romans 8:1 NKJV

All of us have made mistakes. Sometimes our failures result from our own shortsightedness. On other occasions, we are swept up in events that are beyond our abilities to control. Under either set of circumstances, we may experience intense feelings of guilt. But God has an answer for the guilt that we feel. That answer, of course, is His forgiveness.

When we ask our Heavenly Father for His forgiveness, He forgives us completely and without reservation. Then, we must do the difficult work of forgiving ourselves in the same way that God has forgiven us: thoroughly and unconditionally.

If you're feeling guilty, then it's time for a special kind of housecleaning—a housecleaning of your mind and your heart . . . beginning NOW!

More from God's Word

Be diligent to present yourself approved to God, a worker who doesn't need to be ashamed, correctly teaching the word of truth.

2 Timothy 2:15 HCSB

But God, who is abundant in mercy, because of His great love that He had for us, made us alive with the Messiah even though we were dead in trespasses. By grace you are saved!

Ephesians 2:4-5 HCSB

All the prophets testify about Him that through His name everyone who believes in Him will receive forgiveness of sins.

Acts 10:43 HCSB

Blessed be the God and Father of our Lord Jesus Christ, who according to His abundant mercy has begotten us again to a living hope through the resurrection of Jesus Christ from the dead....

1 Peter 1:3 NKJV

More Ideas for Your Journey

Guilt is a gift that leads us to grace.

Franklin Graham

Identify the sin. Confess it. Turn from it. Avoid it at all costs. Live with a clean, forgiven conscience. Don't dwell on what God has forgotten!

Max Lucado

Prayer is essential when a believer is stuck in the pits of unresolved guilt.

Charles Stanley

A Father's Prayer

Dear Lord, thank You for the guilt that I feel when I disobey You. Help me confess my wrongdoings, help me accept Your forgiveness, and help me renew my passion to serve You. Amen

Beyond the Mistakes

Instead, God has chosen the world's foolish things to shame the wise, and God has chosen the world's weak things to shame the strong.

1 Corinthians 1:27 HCSB

As parents, we are far from perfect. And, without question, our children are imperfect as well. Thus, we are imperfect parents raising imperfect children, and, as a result, mistakes are bound to happen.

Has someone in your family experienced a recent setback? If so, it's time to start looking for the lesson that God is trying to teach. It's time to learn what needs to be learned, change what needs to be changed, and move on.

You and your loved ones should view mistakes as opportunities to reassess God's will for your lives. And while you're at it, you should consider life's inevitable disappointments to be powerful opportunities to learn more—more about yourselves, more about your circumstances, and more about your world.

More Ideas for Your Journey

Truth will sooner come out of error than from confusion.

Francis Bacon

Lord, when we are wrong, make us willing to change; and when we are right, make us easy to live with.

Peter Marshall

I hope you don't mind me telling you all this. One can learn only by seeing one's mistakes.

C. S. Lewis

A Father's Prayer

Dear Lord, there's a right way to do things and a wrong way to do things. When I do things that are wrong, help me be quick to ask for forgiveness . . . and quick to correct my mistakes. Amen

God's Guidance

In all your ways acknowledge Him, and He shall direct your paths.

Proverbs 3:6 NKJV

The Bible promises that God will guide you if you let Him. Your job, of course, is to let Him. But sometimes, you will be tempted to do otherwise. Sometimes, you'll be tempted to go along with the crowd; other times, you'll be tempted to do things your way, not God's way. When you feel those temptations, resist them.

What will you allow to guide you through the coming day: your own desires (or, for that matter, the desires of your friends)? Or will you allow God to lead the way? The answer should be obvious. You should let God be your guide. When you entrust your life to Him completely and without reservation, God will give you the strength to meet any challenge, the courage to face any trial, and the wisdom to live in His righteousness. So trust Him today and seek His guidance. When you do, your next step will be the right one.

More from God's Word

Yet Lord, You are our Father; we are the clay, and You are our potter; we all are the work of Your hands.

Isaiah 64:8 HCSB

Lord, You are my lamp; the Lord illuminates my darkness.

2 Samuel 22:29 HCSB

Teach me Your way, Lord, and I will live by Your truth. Give me an undivided mind to fear Your name.

Psalm 86:11 HCSB

But the wisdom from above is first pure, then peace-loving, gentle, compliant, full of mercy and good fruits, without favoritism and hypocrisy.

James 3:17 HCSB

The Lord says, "I will make you wise and show you where to go. I will guide you and watch over you."

Psalm 32:8 NCV

More Ideas for Your Journey

Fix your eyes upon the Lord! Do it once. Do it daily. Do it constantly. Look at the Lord and keep looking at Him.

Charles Swindoll

God's plan for our guidance is for us to grow gradually in wisdom before we get to the crossroads.

Bill Hybels

We must always invite Jesus to be the navigator of our plans, desires, wills, and emotions, for He is the way, the truth, and the life.

Bill Bright

A Father's Prayer

Dear Lord, thank You for Your constant presence and Your constant love. I draw near to You this day with the confidence that You are ready to guide me. Help me walk closely with You, Father, and help me share Your Good News with all who cross my path. Amen

Getting It Done Now

When you make a vow to God, don't delay fulfilling it, because He does not delight in fools. Fulfill what you vow.

Ecclesiastes 5:4 HCSB

The old saying is both familiar and true: actions speak louder than words. And as believers, we must beware: our actions should always give credence to the changes that Christ can make in the lives of those who walk with Him.

God calls upon each of us to act in accordance with His will and with respect for His commandments. If we are to be responsible believers, we must realize that it is never enough simply to hear the instructions of God; we must also live by them. And it is never enough to wait idly by while others do God's work here on earth; we, too, must act. Doing God's work is a responsibility that each of us must bear, and when we do, our loving Heavenly Father rewards our efforts with a bountiful harvest.

More from God's Word

But be doers of the word and not hearers only.

James 1:22 HCSB

Therefore, get your minds ready for action, being self-disciplined, and set your hope completely on the grace to be brought to you at the revelation of Jesus Christ.

1 Peter 1:13 HCSB

For the hearers of the law are not righteous before God, but the doers of the law will be declared righteous.

Romans 2:13 HCSB

Well done, good and faithful servant; you were faithful over a few things, I will make you ruler over many things. Enter into the joy of your lord.

Matthew 25:21 NKJV

For the Kingdom of God is not just fancy talk; it is living by God's power.

1 Corinthians 4:20 NLT

More Ideas for Your Journey

Do noble things, do not dream them all day long.

Charles Kingsley

Now is the only time worth having because, indeed, it is the only time we have.

C. H. Spurgeon

Every time you refuse to face up to life and its problems, you weaken your character.

E. Stanley Jones

A Father's Prayer

Dear Lord, today is a new day. Help me tackle the important tasks immediately, even if those tasks are unpleasant. Don't let me put off until tomorrow what I should do today. Amen

Time for Family

We can't afford to waste a minute, must not squander these precious daylight hours in frivolity and indulgence, in sleeping around and dissipation, in bickering and grabbing everything in sight. Get out of bed and get dressed! Don't loiter and linger, waiting until the very last minute. Dress yourselves in Christ, and be up and about!

Romans 13:13-14 MSG

It takes time to build strong family ties . . . lots of time. Yet we live in a world where time seems to be an ever-shrinking commodity as we rush from place to place with seldom a moment to spare.

Has the busy pace of life robbed you of sufficient time with your loved ones? If so, it's time to fine-tune your priorities. And God can help.

When you make God a full partner in every aspect of your life, He will lead you along the proper path: His path. When you allow God to reign over your life, He will enrich your relationships and your life. So, as you plan for the day ahead, make God's priorities your priorities. When you do, every other priority will have a tendency to fall neatly into place.

More Ideas for Your Journey

I don't buy the cliché that quality time is the most important thing. If you don't have enough quantity, you won't get quality.

Leighton Ford

The more time you give to something, the more you reveal its importance and value to you.

Rick Warren

What really builds togetherness is time spent together—lots of time.

Dennis Swanberg

A Father's Prayer

Dear Lord, You have given me a wonderful gift: time here on earth. Let me use it wisely—for the glory of Your kingdom and the betterment of my family—today and every day that I live. Amen

Big Plans

Teach me to do Your will, for You are my God. May Your gracious Spirit lead me on level ground.

Psalm 143:10 HCSB

The Bible makes it clear: God has plans—very big plans—for you and your family. But He won't force His plans upon you—if you wish to experience the abundance that God has in store, you must be willing to accept His will and follow His Son.

As Christians, you and your family members should ask yourselves this question: "How closely can we make our plans match God's plans?" The more closely you manage to follow the path that God intends for your lives, the better.

Do you and your loved ones have questions or concerns about the future? Take them to God in prayer. Do you have hopes and expectations? Talk to God about your dreams. Are you and your family members carefully planning for the days and weeks ahead? Consult God as you establish your priorities. Turn every concern over to your Heavenly Father, and sincerely seek His guidance—prayerfully, earnestly, and often. Then, listen for His answers . . . and trust the answers that He gives.

More from God's Word

We know that all things work together for the good of those who love God: those who are called according to His purpose.

Romans 8:28 HCSB

But as for you, you meant evil against me; but God meant it for good, in order to bring it about as it is this day, to save many people alive.

Genesis 50:20 NKJV

A man's heart plans his way, but the Lord directs his steps.

Proverbs 16:9 NKJV

For My thoughts are not your thoughts, nor are your ways My ways, says the LORD. "For as the heavens are higher than the earth, so are My ways higher than your ways, and My thoughts than your thoughts."

Isaiah 55:8-9 NKJV

More Ideas for Your Journey

The Almighty does nothing without reason, although the frail mind of man cannot explain the reason.

St. Augustine

Faith never knows where it is being led, but it loves the One who is leading.

Oswald Chambers

One of the wonderful things about being a Christian is the knowledge that God has a plan for our lives.

Warren Wiersbe

A Father's Prayer

Dear Lord, I will seek Your plan for my life. Even when I don't understand why things happen, I will trust You. Even when I am uncertain of my next step, I will trust You. There are many things that I cannot do, Lord, and there are many things that I cannot understand. But one thing I can do is to trust You always. And I will. Amen

So Laugh!

Laugh with your happy friends when they're happy; share tears when they're down.

Romans 12:15 MSG

Laughter is a gift from God, a gift that He intends for us to use. Yet sometimes, because of the inevitable stresses of everyday living, we fail to find the fun in life. When we allow life's inevitable disappointments to cast a pall over our lives and our souls, we do a profound disservice to ourselves and to our loved ones.

If you've allowed the clouds of life to obscure the blessings of life, perhaps you've formed the unfortunate habit of taking things just a little too seriously. If so, it's time to fret a little less and laugh a little more.

So today, look for the humor that most certainly surrounds you—when you do, you'll find it. And remember: God created laughter for a reason...and Father indeed knows best. So laugh!

More Ideas for Your Journey

Laughter is like premium gasoline: It takes the knock out of living.

Anonymous

I think everybody ought to be a laughing Christian. I'm convinced that there's just one place where there's not any laughter, and that's hell.

Jerry Clower

If you want people to feel comfortable around you, to enjoy being with you, then learn to laugh at yourself and find humor in life's little mishaps.

Dennis Swanberg

A Father's Prayer

Lord, when I begin to take myself or my life too seriously, let me laugh. When I rush from place to place, slow me down, Lord, and let me laugh. Put a smile on my face, Dear Lord, and let me share that smile with all who cross my path . . . and let me laugh. Amen

Let God Judge

Do not judge, and you will not be judged. Do not condemn, and you will not be condemned. Forgive, and you will be forgiven.

Luke 6:37 HCSB

We have all fallen short of God's commandments, and He has forgiven us. We, too, must forgive others. And, we must refrain from judging them.

Are you one of those people who finds it easy to judge others? If so, it's time to change.

God does not need (or, for that matter, want) your help. Why? Because God is perfectly capable of judging the human heart . . . while you are not.

As Christians, we are warned that to judge others is to invite fearful consequences. To the extent we judge others, so, too, will we be judged by God. Let us refrain, then, from judging our neighbors. Instead, let us forgive them and love them in the same way that God has forgiven us.

More from God's Word

Speak and act as those who will be judged by the law of freedom. For judgment is without mercy to the one who hasn't shown mercy. Mercy triumphs over judgment.

James 2:12-13 HCSB

When Jesus stood up, He said to her, "Woman, where are they? Has no one condemned you?" "No one, Lord," she answered. "Neither do I condemn you," said Jesus. "Go, and from now on do not sin any more."

John 8:10-11 HCSB

How can you say to your brother, "Brother, let me take out the speck that is in your eye," when you yourself don't see the log in your eye? Hypocrite! First take the log out of your eye, and then you will see clearly to take out the speck in your brother's eye.

Luke 6:42 HCSB

Therefore judge nothing before the time, until the Lord comes, who will both bring to light the hidden things of darkness and reveal the counsels of the hearts. Then each one's praise will come from God.

1 Corinthians 4:5 NKJV

More Ideas for Your Journey

An individual Christian may see fit to give up all sorts of things for special reasons—marriage, or meat, or beer, or cinema; but the moment he starts saying these things are bad in themselves, or looking down his nose at other people who do use them, he has taken the wrong turn.

C. S. Lewis

Don't judge other people more harshly than you want God to judge you.

Marie T. Freeman

Christians think they are prosecuting attorneys or judges, when, in reality, God has called all of us to be witnesses.

Warren Wiersbe

A Father's Prayer

Dear Lord, sometimes I am quick to judge others. But, You have commanded me not to judge. Keep me mindful, Father, that when I judge others, I am living outside of Your will for my life. You have forgiven me, Lord. Let me forgive others, let me love them, and let me help them . . . without judging them. Amen

On Guard Against Evil

Be sober! Be on the alert! Your adversary the Devil is prowling around like a roaring lion, looking for anyone he can devour.

1 Peter 5:8 HCSB

Nineteenth-century clergyman Edwin Hubbel Chapin warned, "Neutral men are the devil's allies." His words were true then, and they're true now. Neutrality in the face of evil is a sin. Yet all too often, we fail to fight evil, not because we are neutral, but because we are shortsighted: we don't fight the devil because we don't recognize his handiwork.

If we are to recognize evil and fight it, we must pay careful attention. We must pay attention to God's Word, and we must pay attention to the realities of everyday life. When we observe life objectively, and when we do so with eyes and hearts that are attuned to God's Holy Word, we can no longer be neutral believers. And when we are no longer neutral, God rejoices while the devil despairs.

More from God's Word

Therefore, submit to God. But resist the Devil, and he will flee from you. Draw near to God, and He will draw near to you. Cleanse your hands, sinners, and purify your hearts, double-minded people!

James 4:7-8 HCSB

For everyone who practices wicked things hates the light and avoids it, so that his deeds may not be exposed. But anyone who lives by the truth comes to the light, so that his works may be shown to be accomplished by God.

John 3:20–21 HCSB

Don't consider yourself to be wise; fear the Lord and turn away from evil.

Proverbs 3:7 HCSB

But the path of the just is like the shining sun, that shines ever brighter unto the perfect day. The way of the wicked is like darkness; they do not know what makes them stumble.

Proverbs 4:18-19 NKJV

Do not be conquered by evil, but conquer evil with good.

Romans 12:21 HCSB

More Ideas for Your Journey

Of two evils, choose neither.

C. H. Spurgeon

Christianity isn't a religion about going to Sunday school, potluck suppers, being nice, holding car washes, sending your secondhand clothes off to Mexico—as good as those things might be. This is a world at war.

John Eldredge

God loves you, and He yearns for you to turn away from the path of evil. You need His forgiveness, and you need Him to come into your life and remake you from within.

Billy Graham

A Father's Prayer

Lord, strengthen my walk with You. Evil comes in many disguises, and sometimes it is only with Your help that I can recognize right from wrong. Your presence in my life enables me to choose truth and to live a life pleasing to You. May I always live in Your presence. Amen

Rejoice Now!

Rejoice in the Lord always. I will say it again: Rejoice!

Philippians 4:4 HCSB

Have you made the choice to rejoice? Hopefully so. After all, if you're a believer, you have plenty of reasons to be joyful. Yet sometimes, amid the inevitable hustle and bustle of life, you may lose sight of your blessings as you wrestle with the challenges of everyday life.

Christ made it clear to His followers: He intended that His joy would become their joy. And it still holds true today: Christ intends that His believers share His love with His joy in their hearts.

What does life have in store for you? A world full of possibilities (of course it's up to you to seize them) and God's promise of abundance (of course it's up to you to accept it). So, as you embark upon the next phase of your journey, remember to celebrate the life that God has given you. Your Creator has blessed you beyond measure. Honor Him with your prayers, your words, your deeds, and your joy.

More from God's Word

So you also have sorrow now. But I will see you again. Your hearts will rejoice, and no one will rob you of your joy.

John 16:22 HCSB

Make me to hear joy and gladness.

Psalm 51:8 KJV

Now I am coming to You, and I speak these things in the world so that they may have My joy completed in them.

John 17:13 HCSB

But let all who take refuge in You rejoice.

Psalm 5:11 HCSB

Weeping may spend the night, but there is joy in the morning.

Psalm 30:5 HCSB

More Ideas for Your Journey

Christ and joy go together.

E. Stanley Jones

Joy is the serious business of heaven.

C. S. Lewis

As Catherine of Siena said, "All the way to heaven is heaven." A joyful end requires a joyful means. Bless the Lord.

Eugene Peterson

A Father's Prayer

Dear Lord, You have given me so many blessings; let me celebrate Your gifts. Make me thankful, loving, responsible, and wise. I praise You, Father, for the gift of Your Son and for the priceless gift of salvation. Make me be a joyful Christian and a worthy example to my loved ones, today and every day. Amen

Imitating the Master

Therefore, be imitators of God, as dearly loved children.

Ephesians 5:1 HCSB

I mitating Christ is impossible, but attempting to imitate Him is both possible and advisable. By attempting to imitate Jesus, we seek, to the best of our abilities, to walk in His footsteps. To the extent we succeed in following Him, we receive the spiritual abundance that is the rightful possession of those who love Christ and keep His commandments.

Do you seek God's blessings for the day ahead? Then, to the best of your abilities, imitate His Son. You will fall short, of course. But if your heart is right and your intentions are pure, God will bless your efforts, your day, and your life.

More from God's Word

But whoever keeps His word, truly the love of God is perfected in him. By this we know that we are in Him. He who says he abides in Him ought himself also to walk just as He walked.

1 John 2:5-6 NKJV

Whoever serves me must follow me. Then my servant will be with me everywhere I am. My Father will honor anyone who serves me.

John 12:26 NCV

Then Jesus spoke to them again: "I am the light of the world. Anyone who follows Me will never walk in the darkness, but will have the light of life."

John 8:12 HCSB

Whoever is not willing to carry the cross and follow me is not worthy of me. Those who try to hold on to their lives will give up true life. Those who give up their lives for me will hold on to true life.

Matthew 10:38-39 NCV

More Ideas for Your Journey

Christlikeness is not produced by imitation, but by inhabitation.

Rick Warren

Every Christian is to become a little Christ. The whole purpose of becoming a Christian is simply nothing else.

C. S. Lewis

A person who gazes and keeps on gazing at Jesus becomes like him in appearance.

E. Stanley Jones

A Father's Prayer

Dear Jesus, because I am Your disciple, I will trust You, I will obey Your teachings, and I will share Your Good News. You have given me life abundant and life eternal, and I will follow You today and forever. Amen

When You Have Doubts

An indecisive man is unstable in all his ways.

James 1:8 HCSB

If you're a dad who's never had any doubts about his faith, you can stop reading this page now and skip to the next. But if you've ever been plagued by doubts about your faith or your God, keep reading.

Even some of the most faithful Christians are, at times, beset by occasional bouts of discouragement and doubt. But even when we feel far removed from God, God is never far removed from us. He is always with us, always willing to calm the storms of life—always willing to replace our doubts with comfort and assurance.

Whenever you're plagued by doubts, that's precisely the moment you should seek God's presence by genuinely seeking to establish a deeper, more meaningful relationship with His Son. Then you may rest assured that in time, God will calm your fears, answer your prayers, and restore your confidence.

More Ideas for Your Journey

Doubt may not always be a sign that a man is wrong; it may be a sign that he is thinking.

Oswald Chambers

We basically have two choices to make in dealing with the mysteries of God. We can wrestle with Him or we can rest in Him.

Calvin Miller

There is a difference between doubt and unbelief. Doubt is a matter of mind: we cannot understand what God is doing or why He is doing it. Unbelief is a matter of will: we refuse to believe God's Word and obey what He tells us to do.

Warren Wiersbe

A Father's Prayer

Dear God, sometimes this world can be a puzzling place, filled with uncertainty and doubt. When I am unsure of my next step, keep me mindful that You are always near and that You can overcome any challenge. Give me faith, Father, and let me remember always that with Your love and Your power, I can live courageously and faithfully today and every day. Amen

Your Real Treasures

The Lord bless you and keep you; the Lord make His face shine upon you, and be gracious to you.

Numbers 6:24-25 NKJV

Because you are a father, you have been specially blessed by God. God has given you blessings that are too numerous to count. Your blessings include life, family, freedom, friends, talents, and possessions, for starters. But, your greatest blessing—a gift that is yours for the asking—is God's gift of salvation through Christ Jesus.

The gifts you receive from God are multiplied when you share them with others. Today, give thanks to God for your blessings and demonstrate your gratitude by sharing those blessings with your family and with the world.

More from God's Word

You will show me the path of life; in Your presence is fullness of joy; at Your right hand are pleasures forevermore.

Psalm 16:11 NKJV

I will make them and the area around My hill a blessing: I will send down showers in their season—showers of blessing.

Ezekiel 34:26 HCSB

Obey My voice, and I will be your God, and you shall be my people. And walk in all the ways that I have commanded you, that it may be well with you.

Jeremiah 7:23 NKJV

I have come that they may have life, and that they may have it more abundantly.

John 10:10 NKJV

Until now you have asked for nothing in My name. Ask and you will receive, that your joy may be complete.

John 16:24 HCSB

More Ideas for Your Journey

Think of the blessings we so easily take for granted: Life itself; preservation from danger; every bit of health we enjoy; every hour of liberty; the ability to see, to hear, to speak, to think, and to imagine all this comes from the hand of God.

Billy Graham

Blessings can either humble us and draw us closer to God or allow us to become full of pride and self-sufficiency.

Jim Cymbala

God's kindness is not like the sunset—brilliant in its intensity, but dying every second. God's generosity keeps coming and coming and coming.

Bill Hybels

A Father's Prayer

Today, Lord, I count my many blessings, beginning with my family. You have cared for me, Lord, and I will give thanks and praise You always. Today, let me share Your gifts with others, just as You first shared them with me. Amen

Healthy Habits

Do you not know that your body is a sanctuary of the Holy Spirit who is in you, whom you have from God? You are not your own, for you were bought at a price; therefore glorify God in your body.

1 Corinthians 6:19-20 HCSB

It's an old saying and a true one: First, you make your habits, and then your habits make you. Some habits will inevitably bring you closer to God; other habits will lead you away from the path He has chosen for you. If you sincerely desire to improve your spiritual health, you must honestly examine the habits that make up the fabric of your day. And you must abandon those habits that are displeasing to God.

If you trust God, and if you keep asking for His help, He can transform your life. If you sincerely ask Him to help you, the same God who created the universe will help you defeat the harmful habits that have heretofore defeated you. So, if at first you don't succeed, keep praying. God is listening, and He's ready to help you become a better person if you ask Him . . . so ask today.

More from God's Word

Do not be deceived: "Evil company corrupts good habits."

1 Corinthians 15:33 NKJV

Guard your heart above all else, for it is the source of life.

Proverbs 4:23 HCSB

For we know that if our earthly house, a tent, is destroyed, we have a building from God, a house not made with hands, eternal in the heavens.

2 Corinthians 5:1 HCSB

For You formed my inward parts; You covered me in my mother's womb. I will praise You, for I am fearfully and wonderfully made; marvelous are Your works.

Psalm 139:13-14 NKJV

Don't copy the behavior and customs of this world, but let God transform you into a new person by changing the way you think. Then you will know what God wants you to do, and you will know how good and pleasing and perfect his will really is.

Romans 12:2 NLT

More Ideas for Your Journey

You will never change your life until you change something you do daily.

John Maxwell

The simple fact is that if we sow a lifestyle that is in direct disobedience to God's revealed Word, we ultimately reap disaster.

Charles Swindoll

Since behaviors become habits, make them work with you and not against you.

E. Stanley Jones

A Father's Prayer

Dear Lord, help me break bad habits and form good ones. And let my actions be pleasing to You, today and every day. Amen

Observing the Sabbath

Remember the Sabbath day, to keep it holy.

Exodus 20:8 NKJV

When God gave Moses the Ten Commandments, it became perfectly clear that our Heavenly Father intends for us to make the Sabbath a holy day, a day for worship, for contemplation, for fellowship, and for rest. Yet we live in a seven-day-a-week world, a world that all too often treats Sunday as a regular workday.

How does your family observe the Lord's day? When church is over, do you treat Sunday like any other day of the week? If so, it's time to think long and hard about your family's schedule and your family's priorities.

Whenever we ignore God's commandments, we pay a price. So if you've been treating Sunday as just another day, it's time to break that habit. When Sunday rolls around, don't try to fill every spare moment. Take time to rest . . . Father's orders!

More Ideas for Your Journey

Worship is not taught from the pulpit. It must be learned in the heart.

Jim Elliot

Worship is a daunting task. Each worships differently. But each should worship.

Max Lucado

There is no division into sacred and secular; it is all one great, glorious life.

Oswald Chambers

A Father's Prayer

Dear Lord, I thank You for the Sabbath day, a day when my family and I can worship You and praise Your Son. We will keep the Sabbath as a holy day, a day when we can honor You. Amen

Your Thoughts

Fix your thoughts on what is true and honorable and right.
Think about things that are pure and lovely and admirable.
Think about things that are excellent and worthy of praise.

Philippians 4:8 NLT

Thoughts are intensely powerful things. Our thoughts have the power to lift us up or drag us down; they have the power to energize us or deplete us, to inspire us to greater accomplishments or to make those accomplishments impossible.

How will you and your family members direct your thoughts today? Will you obey the words of Philippians 4:8 by dwelling upon those things that are honorable, true, and worthy of praise? Or will you allow your thoughts to be hijacked by the negativity that seems to dominate our troubled world?

Are you fearful, angry, bored, or worried? Are you so preoccupied with the concerns of this day that you fail to thank God for the promise of eternity? Are you confused, bitter, or pessimistic? If so, God wants to have a little talk with you.

God intends that you experience joy and abundance, but He will not force His joy upon you; you must claim it for yourself. It's up to you and your loved ones to celebrate the life that God has given you by focusing your minds upon "whatever is commendable." So form the habit of spending more time thinking about your blessings and less time fretting about your hardships. Then, take time to thank the Giver of all things good for gifts that are, in truth, far too numerous to count.

More from God's Word

Set your minds on what is above, not on what is on the earth.
Colossians 3:2 HCSB

Commit your works to the Lord, and your thoughts will be established.
Proverbs 16:3 NKJV

Guard your heart above all else, for it is the source of life.
Proverbs 4:23 HCSB

May the words of my mouth and the meditation of my heart be acceptable to You, Lord, my rock and my Redeemer.
Psalm 19:14 HCSB

More Ideas for Your Journey

The mind is like a clock that is constantly running down. It has to be wound up daily with good thoughts.

Fulton J. Sheen

God's cure for evil thinking is to fill our minds with that which is good.

George Sweeting

Your thoughts are the determining factor as to whose mold you are conformed to. Control your thoughts and you control the direction of your life.

Charles Stanley

A Father's Prayer

Dear Lord, I will focus on Your love, Your power, Your promises, and Your Son. When I am weak, I will turn to You for strength; when I am worried, I will turn to You for comfort; when I am troubled, I will turn to You for patience and perspective. Help me guard my thoughts, Lord, so that I may honor You this day and forever. Amen

The Gift of Eternal Life

Jesus said to her, "I am the resurrection and the life. The one who believes in Me, even if he dies, will live. Everyone who lives and believes in Me will never die—ever. Do you believe this?"

John 11:25-26 HCSB

Your ability to envision the future, like your life here on earth, is limited. God's vision, however, is not burdened by any such limitations. He sees all things, He knows all things, and His plans for you extend throughout eternity.

God's plans are not limited to the events of daily life. Your Heavenly Father has bigger things in mind for you . . . much bigger things. So praise the Creator for the gift of eternal life and share the Good News with all who cross your path. And remember: if you have given your heart to the Son, you belong to the Father—today, tomorrow, and for all eternity.

More from God's Word

And this is the testimony: God has given us eternal life, and this life is in His Son. The one who has the Son has life. The one who doesn't have the Son of God does not have life. I have written these things to you who believe in the name of the Son of God, so that you may know that you have eternal life.

1 John 5:11-13 HCSB

We do not want you to be uninformed, brothers, concerning those who are asleep, so that you will not grieve like the rest, who have no hope. Since we believe that Jesus died and rose again, in the same way God will bring with Him those who have fallen asleep through Jesus.

1 Thessalonians 4:13-14 HCSB

Pursue righteousness, godliness, faith, love, endurance, and gentleness. Fight the good fight for the faith; take hold of eternal life, to which you were called and have made a good confession before many witnesses.

1 Timothy 6:11-12 HCSB

More Ideas for Your Journey

Someday you will read in the papers that Moody is dead. Don't you believe a word of it. At that moment I shall be more alive than I am now. I was born of the flesh in 1837, I was born of the spirit in 1855. That which is born of the flesh may die. That which is born of the Spirit shall live forever.

D. L. Moody

God loves you and wants you to experience peace and life—abundant and eternal.

Billy Graham

Teach us to set our hopes on heaven, to hold firmly to the promise of eternal life, so that we can withstand the struggles and storms of this world.

Max Lucado

A Father's Prayer

Lord, I am only here on this earth for a brief while. But, You have offered me the priceless gift of eternal life through Your Son Jesus. I accept Your gift, Lord, with thanksgiving and praise. Let me share the good news of my salvation with those who need Your healing touch. Amen

Finding Hope

Now may the God of hope fill you with all joy and peace in believing, so that you may overflow with hope by the power of the Holy Spirit.

Romans 15:13 HCSB

A re you a hope-filled father? You should be. After all, God is good; His love endures; and He has offered you the priceless gift of eternal life.

But sometimes hope slips away, even for the most optimistic pops. Despite God's promises, despite Christ's love, and despite our countless blessings, we can still fall prey to discouragement and doubt. When we do, we need the encouragement of fellow believers, the life-changing power of prayer, and the healing truth of God's Holy Word.

If you find yourself falling into the spiritual traps of worry and discouragement, seek the healing touch of Jesus and the encouraging words of fellow Christians. If you find a friend in need, remind him or her of the peace that is found through a personal relationship with Christ. This world can be a place of trials and tribulations, but as believers, we are secure. God has promised us peace, joy, and eternal life. And, of course, God keeps His promises today, tomorrow, and forever.

More from God's Word

But if we hope for what we do not see, we eagerly wait for it with patience.

Romans 8:25 HCSB

Rejoice in hope; be patient in affliction; be persistent in prayer.

Romans 12:12 HCSB

Lord, I turn my hope to You. My God, I trust in You. Do not let me be disgraced; do not let my enemies gloat over me.

Psalms 25:1-2 HCSB

Let us hold on to the confession of our hope without wavering, for He who promised is faithful.

Hebrews 10:23 HCSB

I wait for the Lord; I wait, and put my hope in His word.

Psalm 130:5 HCSB

More Ideas for Your Journey

Faith looks back and draws courage; hope looks ahead and keeps desire alive.

John Eldredge

If your hopes are being disappointed just now, it means that they are being purified.

Oswald Chambers

The hope we have in Jesus is the anchor for the soul—something sure and steadfast, preventing drifting or giving way, lowered to the depth of God's love.

Franklin Graham

A Father's Prayer

Today, Dear Lord, I will live in hope. If I become discouraged, I will turn to You. If I grow weary, I will seek strength in You. In every aspect of my life, I will trust You. You are my Father, Lord, and I place my hope and my faith in You. Amen

The Best Policy

*The just man walketh in his integrity: his children are blessed
after him.*

Proverbs 20:7 KJV

It has been said on many occasions and in many ways
that honesty is the best policy. For believers, it is far
more important to note that honesty is God's policy.
And if we are to be servants worthy of Jesus Christ, we
must be honest and forthright in our communications
with others. Sometimes, honesty is difficult; sometimes,
honesty is painful; sometimes, honesty is inconvenient;
but always honesty is God's commandment.

In the Book of Proverbs, we read, "The Lord de-
tests lying lips, but he delights in men who are truthful"
(12:22 NIV). Clearly, we must strive to be men whose
words are pleasing to our Creator. Truth is God's way,
and it must be our way, too, even when telling the truth
is difficult. As loving fathers, we can do no less.

More from God's Word

These are the things you must do: Speak truth to one another; render honest and peaceful judgments in your gates.

Zechariah 8:16 HCSB

Ye shall not steal, neither deal falsely, neither lie one to another.

Leviticus 19:11 KJV

The one who lives with integrity lives securely, but whoever perverts his ways will be found out.

Proverbs 10:9 HCSB

The one who lives with integrity will be helped, but one who distorts right and wrong will suddenly fall.

Proverbs 28:18 HCSB

If your life honors the name of Jesus, he will honor you.

2 Thessalonians 1:12 MSG

More Ideas for Your Journey

Integrity is not a given factor in everyone's life. It is a result of self-discipline, inner trust, and a decision to be relentlessly honest in all situations in our lives.

John Maxwell

God doesn't expect you to be perfect, but he does insist on complete honesty.

Rick Warren

A little lie is like a little pregnancy. It doesn't take long before everyone knows.

C. S. Lewis

A Father's Prayer

Heavenly Father, You instruct Your children to seek truth and to live righteously. Help me always to live according to Your commandments. Sometimes, Lord, speaking the truth is difficult, but let me always speak truthfully and forthrightly. And, let me walk righteously and courageously so that others might see Your Grace reflected in my words and my deeds. Amen

God's Timetable

*Wait for the Lord; be courageous and let your heart be strong.
Wait for the Lord.*

Psalm 27:14 HCSB

Are you anxious for God to work out His plan for your life? Who isn't? As believers, we all want God to do great things for us and through us, and we want Him to do those things now. But sometimes, God has other plans. Sometimes, God's timetable does not coincide with our own. It's worth noting, however, that God's timetable is always perfect.

The next time you find your patience tested to the limit, remember that the world unfolds according to God's plan, not ours. Sometimes, we must wait patiently, and that's as it should be. After all, think how patient God has been with us.

More from God's Word

He said to them, "It is not for you to know times or periods that the Father has set by His own authority."

Acts 1:7 HCSB

He has made everything appropriate in its time. He has also put eternity in their hearts, but man cannot discover the work God has done from beginning to end.

Ecclesiastes 3:11 HCSB

Therefore the Lord is waiting to show you mercy, and is rising up to show you compassion, for the Lord is a just God. Happy are all who wait patiently for Him.

Isaiah 30:18 HCSB

For My thoughts are not your thoughts, and your ways are not My ways. For as heaven is higher than earth, so My ways are higher than your ways, and My thoughts than your thoughts.

Isaiah 55:8-9 HCSB

I waited patiently for the LORD; and He inclined to me, and heard my cry.

Psalm 40:1 NKJV

More Ideas for Your Journey

God has a designated time when his promise will be fulfilled and the prayer will be answered.

Jim Cymbala

Will not the Lord's time be better than your time?

C. H. Spurgeon

God is in no hurry. Compared to the works of mankind, He is extremely deliberate. God is not a slave to the human clock.

Charles Swindoll

A Father's Prayer

Dear Lord, Your wisdom is infinite, and the timing of Your Heavenly plan is perfect. You have a plan for my life that is grander than I can imagine. When I am impatient, remind me that You are never early or late. You are always on time, Father, so let me trust in You. Amen

Be His Disciple

Then He said to them all, "If anyone wants to come with Me, he must deny himself, take up his cross daily, and follow Me."

Luke 9:23 HCSB

When Jesus addressed His disciples, He warned that each one must, "take up his cross and follow Me." The disciples must have known exactly what the Master meant. In Jesus' day, prisoners were forced to carry their own crosses to the location where they would be put to death. Thus, Christ's message was clear: in order to follow Him, Christ's disciples must deny themselves and, instead, trust Him completely. Nothing has changed since then.

If we are to be disciples of Christ, we must trust Him and place Him at the very center of our beings. Jesus never comes "next." He is always first. The paradox, of course, is that only by sacrificing ourselves to Him do we gain salvation for ourselves.

Do you seek to be a worthy disciple of Christ? Then pick up His cross today and every day that you live. When you do, He will bless you now and forever.

More from God's Word

"Follow Me," Jesus told them, "and I will make you into fishers of men!" Immediately they left their nets and followed Him.

Mark 1:17-18 HCSB

You did not choose Me, but I chose you. I appointed you that you should go out and produce fruit, and that your fruit should remain, so that whatever you ask the Father in My name, He will give you.

John 15:16 HCSB

But whoever keeps His word, truly in him the love of God is perfected. This is how we know we are in Him: the one who says he remains in Him should walk just as He walked.

1 John 2:5-6 HCSB

The one who loves his life will lose it, and the one who hates his life in this world will keep it for eternal life. If anyone serves Me, he must follow Me. Where I am, there My servant also will be. If anyone serves Me, the Father will honor him.

John 12:25-26 HCSB

More Ideas for Your Journey

As we seek to become disciples of Jesus Christ, we should never forget that the word disciple is directly related to the word discipline. To be a disciple of the Lord Jesus Christ is to know his discipline.

Dennis Swanberg

There is not Christianity without a cross, for you cannot be a disciple of Jesus without taking up your cross.

Henry Blackaby

A disciple is a follower of Christ. That means you take on His priorities as your own. His agenda becomes your agenda. His mission becomes your mission.

Charles Stanley

A Father's Prayer

Help me, Lord, to understand what cross I am to bear this day. Give me the strength and the courage to carry that cross along the path of Your choosing so that I may be a worthy disciple of Your Son. Amen

Wisdom Now!

Acquire wisdom—how much better it is than gold! And acquire understanding—it is preferable to silver.

Proverbs 16:16 HCSB

D o you seek wisdom for yourself and for your family? Of course you do. But as a savvy dad, you know that wisdom can be an elusive commodity in today's troubled world. In a society filled with temptations and distractions; it's easy for parents and children alike to stray far from the source of the ultimate wisdom: God's Holy Word.

When you begin a daily study of God's Word and live according to His commandments, you will become wise. But don't expect to open your Bible today and be wise tomorrow. Wisdom is not like a mushroom; it does not spring up overnight. It is, instead, like an oak tree that starts as a tiny acorn, grows into a sapling, and eventually reaches up to the sky, tall and strong.

As a way of understanding God's plan for your life, study His Word and live by it. When you do, you will accumulate a storehouse of wisdom that will enrich your own life and the lives of your family members.

More from God's Word

The fear of the Lord is the beginning of wisdom; a good understanding have all those who do His commandments. His praise endures forever.

Psalm 111:10 NKJV

Therefore, everyone who hears these words of Mine and acts on them will be like a sensible man who built his house on the rock. The rain fell, the rivers rose, and the winds blew and pounded that house. Yet it didn't collapse, because its foundation was on the rock.

Matthew 7:24–25 HCSB

A wise man will hear and increase learning, and a man of understanding will attain wise counsel.

Proverbs 1:5 NKJV

Teach me, O Lord, the way of Your statutes, and I shall keep it to the end.

Psalm 119:33 NKJV

Do you want to be counted wise, to build a reputation for wisdom? Here's what you do: Live well, live wisely, live humbly. It's the way you live, not the way you talk, that counts.

James 3:13 MSG

More Ideas for Your Journey

The more wisdom enters our hearts, the more we will be able to trust our hearts in difficult situations.

John Eldredge

Don't expect wisdom to come into your life like great chunks of rock on a conveyor belt. Wisdom comes privately from God as a by-product of right decisions, godly reactions, and the application of spiritual principles to daily circumstances.

Charles Swindoll

If you lack knowledge, go to school. If you lack wisdom, get on your knees.

Vance Havner

A Father's Prayer

Dear Lord, give me wisdom to love my family, to care for them, and to help them understand the wisdom of Your Holy Word. Let me share Your wisdom by the words I speak and the example that I set, today and every day that I live. Amen

Devotion 100

For God So Loved the World

This is how much God loved the world: He gave his Son, his one and only Son. And this is why: so that no one need be destroyed; by believing in him anyone can have a whole and lasting life.

John 3:16 MSG

Christ sacrificed His life on the cross so that we might have eternal life. This gift, freely given by God's only begotten Son, is the priceless possession of everyone who accepts Him as Lord and Savior. God is waiting patiently for each of us to accept the gift of eternal life. Let us claim Christ's gift today.

It is by God's grace that we have been saved, through faith. We are saved not because of our good deeds but because of our faith in Christ. May we, who have been given so much, praise our Savior for the gift of salvation, and may we share the joyous news of our Master's love and His grace.

More from God's Word

Jesus said to her, "I am the resurrection and the life. The one who believes in Me, even if he dies, will live. Everyone who lives and believes in Me will never die—ever. Do you believe this?"

John 11:25-26 HCSB

I am the door. If anyone enters by Me, he will be saved, and will come in and go out and find pasture.

John 10:9 HCSB

Let it be known to all of you and to all the people of Israel, that by the name of Jesus Christ the Nazarene—whom you crucified and whom God raised from the dead—by Him this man is standing here before you healthy. This Jesus is the stone rejected by you builders, which has become the cornerstone. There is salvation in no one else, for there is no other name under heaven given to people, and we must be saved by it.

Acts 4:10-12 HCSB

Here is a trustworthy saying that deserves full acceptance: Christ Jesus came into the world to save sinners—of whom I am the worst.

1 Timothy 1:15 NIV

More Ideas for Your Journey

God did everything necessary to provide for our forgiveness by sacrificing His perfect, holy Son as the atoning substitute for our sins.

Franklin Graham

The way to be saved is not to delay, but to come and take.

D. L. Moody

The essence of salvation is an about-face from self-centeredness to God-centeredness.

Henry Blackaby

A Father's Prayer

Dear Lord, I am only here on this earth for a brief while. But, You have offered me the priceless gift of eternal life through Your Son Jesus. I accept Your gift, Lord, with thanksgiving and praise. Let me share the Good News of my salvation with all those who need Your healing touch. Amen